The Wisdom of
Adam Smith

The Wisdom of
Adam Smith

Selected by John Haggarty
Edited and with an Introduction by
Benjamin A. Rogge

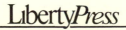

Indianapolis

Liberty Press is a publishing imprint of Liberty Fund, Inc., a foundation established to encourage study of the ideal of a society of free and responsible individuals.

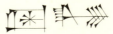

The cuneiform inscription that serves as the design motif for our endpapers is the earliest known written appearance of the word ''freedom'' (*ama-gi*), or liberty. It is taken from a clay document written about 2300 B.C. in the Sumerian city-state of Lagash.

Library of Congress Catalog Card No.: 76-43441
ISBN 0-913966-21-5

Contents

The Wisdom of
Adam Smith

Introduction

Benjamin A. Rogge

In the year 1776, Adam Smith published his *Wealth of Nations*, which, looking at its ultimate results, is probably the most important book that has ever been written.

E ven an admitted Adam Smith buff — as I happily admit to being — may be somewhat embarrassed by this claim made by English historian Henry Thomas Buckle. But that Smith's ideas did have consequences — for the better or for the worse, depending on one's view — cannot be doubted. The world of today is almost certainly somewhat different than it would have been had the gypsy band that held young Adam Smith captive for a brief time never returned him to civilized life.

This adventure with the gypsies may well have been the only pure television material in the whole of Smith's life. He was born in Kirkcaldy, Scotland in 1723 and died in Edinburgh in 1790. In between, he lived a life free of scandal, free of great incident, free of real discomfort or distress, and free of financial embarrassment. It hardly need be added that his life was also free of wife and children. He was a student (at Glasgow and Oxford) and an educator (at Edinburgh and Glasgow) and his friends were scholars and educators — but also artists, writers, businessmen and men of affairs. In a sense, though, he was always the true "spectator" of the human scene, involved in that scene, yes, but always capable of detached analysis and appraisal of everything that came within his view.

His writing is blessedly free of that use of jargon (*and* mathematics) that characterizes most of the modern materials in economics. His ideas are expressed in a lucid, straightforward manner that makes them accessible to all. He was also capable of turning out a magnificently pungent sentence. I offer in witness his description of the likely consequences of inviting the American colonies to send representatives to the British Parliament:

> . . . Instead of piddling for the little prizes which are to be found in what may be called the paltry raffle of colony faction; they might then hope, from the presumption which men naturally have in their own ability and good fortune, to draw some of the great prizes which sometimes come from the wheel of the great state lottery of British politics . . .

It is this combination of wisdom and style, plus the occasion of the 200th birthday of *The Wealth of Nations*, that gives a reason to this (yet another) collection of Smith's words.

The true Smith disciple will be distressed by the fact of abridgment itself and by the choice of passages to be included. To the less demanding, this may well prove to be a less-time-consuming way into Smith's world than the unabridged books and papers. To all who are interested in the possibility of human societies living and prospering with freedom and order, the materials presented here should constitute a gold mine of the quotable.

The final question is, why John Haggarty? Why Haggarty as the person to do the selecting and organizing of an abridged version of the wisdom of Adam Smith? On the surface, he would seem to be a most unlikely candidate for the role. He left school at fourteen and is totally innocent of any classroom exposure to the ideas of either Adam Smith or Karl Marx. Worse yet, he is a member of what Smith called "that most unprosperous race of men" — men of letters. In other words, he lives by and for words. These words he has put into the writing of plays for the theater and of scripts for films and for television. "The greatest thing I ever found out," he says, "was what Plato stated very starkly — 'Words are tools to help us understand.' "

He has been described (in a recent article about him in the *Glasgow Evening Times*) as "of that special breed known as the Inquiring Scot." This, of course, makes him one with Adam Smith. It was my privilege to work with John Haggarty in the making of the documentary film, "Adam Smith and The Wealth of Nations." He was responsible for both script and direction — and a happy choice he proved to be, indeed, in both roles. Three of us from the academic world, three card-carrying, licensed practitioners of the mysterious arts of the economist, were asked to serve as technical advisors in the making of the film. Our assumption was that, at best, the script would be actually written by someone who knew little or nothing about Smith and who would probably be antagonistic to Smith's ideas once he came to know them. By the time our sessions came to an end we were disabused of both of these presumptions.

I say, with no exaggeration, that John Haggarty has become an absolutely first-rate Smith scholar — and, on most issues, a Smith disciple as well. As a zealous and jealous guardian of the true Smith faith, I am pleased to place my unqualified endorsement on Haggarty's work with Smith as reflected in this volume. Without further comment, I bid you to read, to enjoy and to grow in wisdom.

Selector's Note

The quotations in this manuscript are taken
from the Liberty Classics edition of *The Theory
of Moral Sentiments* (Indianapolis, 1976), with an
introduction by E. G. West, and the Modern
Library edition of *The Wealth of Nations*.
Source is indicated by the letters *MS* or
WN followed by the page numbers.

        — John Haggarty

1

Education

The great secret of education is to direct vanity to proper objects.

MS 417

There is scarce any man . . . who by discipline, education, and example, may not be so impressed with a regard to general rules, as to act upon almost every occasion with tolerable decency, and through the whole of his life to avoid any considerable degree of blame.

MS 270

Before the invention of the art of printing, a scholar and a beggar seem to have been terms very nearly synonymous.

WN 132

The endowments of schools and colleges have necessarily diminished more or less the necessity of application in the teachers. Their subsistence, so far as it arises from their salaries, is evidently derived from a fund altogether independent of their success and reputation in their particular professions.

WN 717

If the teacher happens to be a man of sense, it must be an unpleasant thing to him to be conscious, while he is lecturing his students, that he is either speaking or reading nonsense, or what is very little better than nonsense. It must, too, be unpleasant to him to observe that the greater part of his students desert his lectures, or perhaps attend upon them with plain enough marks of neglect, contempt, and derision. If he is obliged, therefore, to give a certain number of lectures, these motives alone, without any other interest, might dispose him to take some pains to give tolerably good ones. Several different expedients, however, may be fallen upon which will effectually blunt the edge of all those incitements to diligence. The teacher, instead of explaining to his pupils himself the science in which he proposes to instruct them, may read some book upon it; and if this book is written in a foreign and dead language, by interpreting it to them into their own; or, what would give him still less trouble, by making them interpret it to him, and by now and then making an occasional remark upon it, he may flatter himself that he is giving a lecture. The slightest degree of knowledge and application will enable him to do this without exposing himself to contempt or derision, or saying anything that is really foolish, absurd, or ridiculous. The discipline of the college, at the same time, may enable him to force all his pupils to the most regular attendance upon this sham lecture, and to maintain the most decent and respectful behaviour during the whole time of the performance.

WN 720

The discipline of colleges and universities is in general contrived, not for the benefit of the students, but for the interest, or more properly speaking, for the ease of the masters. Its object is, in all cases, to maintain the authority of the master, and whether he neglects or performs his duty, to oblige the students in all cases to behave to him as if he performed it with the greatest diligence and ability. It seems to presume perfect wisdom and virtue in the one order, and the greatest weakness and folly in the other. Where the masters, however, really perform their duty, there are no examples, I believe, that the greater part of the students ever neglect theirs. No discipline is ever requisite to force attendance upon lectures which are really worth the attending, as is well known wherever any such lectures are given.

WN 720, 721

Those parts of education, it is to be observed, for the teaching of which there are no public institutions, are generally the best taught. When a young man goes to a fencing or a dancing school, he does not indeed always learn to fence or to dance very well; but he seldom fails of learning to fence or to dance.

WN 721

Were there no public institutions for education, no system, no science would be taught for which there was not some demand; or which the circumstances of the times did not render it either necessary, or convenient, or at least fashionable, to learn. A private teacher could never find his account in teaching, either an exploded and antiquated system of a science acknowledged to be useful, or a science universally believed to be a mere useless and pedantic heap of sophistry and nonsense. Such systems, such sciences, can subsist no where, but in those incorporated societies for education whose prosperity and revenue are in a great measure independent of their reputation, and altogether independent of their industry.

WN 733

Though the common people cannot, in any civilised society, be so well instructed as people of some rank and fortune, the most essential parts of education, however, to read, write, and account, can be acquired at so early a period of life that the greater part even of those who are to be bred to the lowest occupations have time to acquire them before they can be employed in those occupations. For a very small expense the public can facilitate, can encourage, and can even impose upon almost the whole body of the people the necessity of acquiring those most essential parts of education.

WN 737

By sending his son abroad, a father delivers himself at least for some time, from so disagreeable an object as that of a son unemployed, neglected, and going to ruin before his eyes.

WN 728

Do you wish to educate your children to be dutiful to their parents, to be kind and affectionate to their brothers and sisters? Put them under the necessity of being dutiful children, of being kind affectionate brothers and sisters: educate them in your own house. . . . Domestic education is the institution of nature — public education the contrivance of man. It is surely unnecessary to say which is likely to be the wisest.

MS 363, 364

The contempt of risk and the presumptuous hope of success, are in no period of life more active than at the age at which young people choose their professions.

WN 109

2

Art and Aesthetics

In all the liberal and ingenious arts, in painting, in poetry, in music, in eloquence, in philosophy, the great artist feels always the real imperfection of his own best works, and is more sensible than any man how much they fall short of that ideal perfection of which he has formed some conception, which he imitates as well as he can, but which he despairs of ever equalling. It is the inferior artist only who is ever perfectly satisfied with his own performances.

MS 402

It is the acute and delicate discernment of the man of taste, who distinguishes the minute, and scarce perceptible differences of beauty and deformity; it is the comprehensive accuracy of the experienced mathematician, who unravels with ease the most intricate and perplexed proportions; it is the great leader in science and taste, the man who directs and conducts our own sentiments, the extent and superior justness of whose talents astonish us with wonder and surprise, who excites our admiration, and seems to deserve our applause; and upon this foundation is grounded the greater part of the praise which is bestowed upon what are called the intellectual virtues.

MS 64, 65

That utility is one of the principal sources of beauty, has been observed by every body who has considered with any attention what constitutes the nature of beauty. The conveniency of a house gives pleasure to the spectator as well as its regularity; and he is as much hurt when he observes the contrary defect, as when he sees the correspondent windows of different forms, or the door not placed exactly in the middle of the building. That the fitness of any system or machine to produce the end for which it was intended, bestows a certain propriety and beauty upon the whole, and renders the very thought and contemplation of it agreeable, is so very obvious, that nobody has overlooked it.

MS 297

The loss of a leg may generally be regarded as a more real calamity than the loss of a mistress. It would be a ridiculous tragedy, however, of which the catastrophe was to turn upon a loss of that kind. A misfortune of the other kind, how frivolous soever it may appear to be, has given occasion to many a fine one.

MS 79

When we are determining the degree of blame or applause which seems due to any action, we very frequently make use of two different standards. The first is the idea of complete propriety and perfection, which, in those difficult situations, no human conduct ever did, or ever can, come up to; and in comparison with which the actions of all men must for ever appear blameable and imperfect. The second is the idea of that degree of proximity or distance from this complete perfection, which the actions of the greater part of men commonly arrive at. Whatever goes beyond this degree, how far soever it may be removed from absolute perfection, seems to deserve applause; and whatever falls short of it, to deserve blame.

It is in the same manner that we judge of the productions of all the arts which address themselves to the imagination. When a critic examines the work of any of the great masters in poetry or painting, he may sometimes examine it by an idea of perfection, in his own mind, which neither that nor any other human work will ever come up to; and as long as he compares it with this standard, he can see nothing in it but faults and imperfections. But when he comes to consider the rank which it ought to hold among other works of the same kind, he necessarily compares it with a very different standard, the common degree of excellence which is usually attained in this particular art; and when he judges of it by this new measure, it may often appear to deserve the highest applause, upon account of its approaching much nearer to perfection than the greater part of those works which can be brought into competition with it.

MS 73, 74

An eminent artist will bring about a considerable change in the established modes of each of those arts, and introduce a new fashion of writing, music, or architecture. As the dress of an agreeable man of high rank recommends itself, and how peculiar and fantastical soever, comes soon to be admired and imitated; so the excellencies of an eminent master recommend his peculiarities, and his manner becomes the fashionable style in the art which he practises. . . . After the praise of refining the taste of a nation, the highest eulogy, perhaps, which can be bestowed upon any author, is to say that he corrupted it.

MS 323, 324

The exorbitant rewards of players, opera-singers, opera-dancers, etc., are founded upon those two principles; the rarity and beauty of the talents, and the discredit of employing them in this manner.

WN 107

Premiums given by the public to artists and manufacturers who excel in their particular occupations, are not liable to the same objections as bounties. By encouraging extraordinary dexterity and ingenuity, they serve to keep up the emulation of the workmen actually employed in those respective occupations, and are not considerable enough to turn towards any one of them a greater share of the capital of the country than what would go to it of its own accord. Their tendency is not to overturn the natural balance of employments, but to render the work which is done in each as perfect and complete as possible. The expence of premiums, besides, is very trifling; that of bounties very great. The bounty upon corn alone has sometimes cost the public in one year more than three hundred thousand pounds.

Bounties are sometimes called premiums, as drawbacks are sometimes called bounties. But we must in all cases attend to the nature of the thing, without paying any regard to the word.

WN 489, 490

That unprosperous race of men commonly called men of letters . . .

WN 131

3

Philosophy

The most sublime speculation of the contemplative philosopher can scarce compensate the neglect of the smallest active duty.

MS 386

By nature a philosopher is not in genius and disposition half so different from a street porter, as a mastiff is from a greyhound, or a greyhound from a spaniel, or this last from a shepherd's dog.

WN 16

The difference of natural talents in different men is, in reality, much less than we are aware of; and the very different genius which appears to distinguish men of different professions, when grown up to maturity, is not upon many occasions so much the cause as the effect of the division of labour. The difference between the most dissimilar characters, between a philosopher and a common street porter, for example, seems to arise not so much from nature as from habit, custom, and education.

WN 15, 16

The great phenomena of nature — the revolutions of the heavenly bodies, eclipses, comets; thunder, lightning, and other extraordinary meteors; the generation, the life, growth, and dissolution of plants and animals — are objects which, as they necessarily excite the wonder, so they naturally call forth the curiosity, of mankind to inquire into their causes. Superstition first attempted to satisfy this curiosity, by referring all those wonderful appearances to the immediate agency of the gods. Philosophy afterwards endeavoured to account for them from more familiar causes, or from such as mankind were better acquainted with, than the agency of the gods.

WN 723, 724

Are you in adversity? Do not mourn in the darkness of solitude, do not regulate your sorrow according to the indulgent sympathy of your intimate friends; return, as soon as possible, to the daylight of the world and of society.

MS 257

Are you in prosperity? Do not confine the enjoyment of your good fortune to your own house, to the company of your own friends, perhaps of your flatterers, of those who build upon your fortune the hopes of mending their own; frequent those who are independent of you, who can value you only for your character and conduct, and not for your fortune.

MS 257

Society and conversation, therefore, are the most powerful remedies for restoring the mind to its tranquility, if, at any time, it has unfortunately lost it; as well as the best preservatives of that equal and happy temper, which is so necessary to self-satisfaction and enjoyment.

MS 69

The overweening conceit which the greater part of men have of their own abilities is an ancient evil remarked by the philosophers and moralists of all ages. Their absurd presumption in their own good fortune has been less taken notice of. It is, however, if possible, still more universal. There is no man living who, when in tolerable health and spirits, has not some share of it. The chance of gain is by every man more or less over-valued, and the chance of loss is by most men undervalued, and by scarce any man, who is in tolerable health and spirits, valued more than it is worth.

WN 107

A certain reserve is necessary when we talk of our own friends, our own studies, our own professions. All these are objects which we cannot expect should interest our companions in the same degree in which they interest us. And it is for want of this reserve, that the one half of mankind make bad company to the other.

MS 85, 86

Happiness consists in tranquility and enjoyment. Without tranquility there can be no enjoyment; and where there is perfect tranquility there is scarce anything which is not capable of amusing.

MS 250

All the improvements in machinery, however, have by no means been the inventions of those who had occasion to use the machines. Many improvements have been made by the ingenuity of the makers, when to make them became the business of a peculiar trade; and some by that of those who are called philosophers or men of speculation, whose trade it is not to do anything, but to observe everything; and who, upon that account, are often capable of combining together the powers of the most distant and dissimilar objects. In the progress of society, philosophy or speculation becomes, like every other employment, the principal or sole trade and occupation of a particular class of citizens. Like every other employment too, it is subdivided into a great number of different branches, each of which affords occupation to a peculiar tribe or class of philosophers; and this subdivision of employment in philosophy, as well as in every other

business, improves dexterity, and saves time. Each individual becomes more expert in his own peculiar branch,
more work is done upon the whole, and the quantity of
science is considerably increased by it.

WN 10

4

Natural Theology
and Religion

The idea of that divine Being, whose benevolence and wisdom have from all eternity contrived and conducted the immense machine of the universe so as at all times to produce the greatest possible quantity of happiness, is certainly, of all the objects of human contemplation, by far the most sublime. Every other thought necessarily appears mean in the comparison.

MS 385

Self-preservation, and the propagation of the species, are the great ends which nature seems to have proposed in the formation of all animals. Mankind are endowed with a desire of those ends, and an aversion to the contrary; with a love of life, and a dread of dissolution; with a desire of the continuance and perpetuity of the species, and with an aversion to the thoughts of its entire extinction. But though we are in this manner endowed with a very strong desire of those ends, it has not been entrusted to the slow and uncertain determinations of our reason, to find out the proper means of bringing them about. Nature has directed us to the greater part of these by original and immediate instincts. Hunger, thirst, the passion which unites the two sexes, the love of pleasure, and the dread of pain, prompt us to apply those means for their own sakes, and without any consideration of their tendency to those beneficent ends which the great Director of nature intended to produce by them.

MS 152

Religion, even in its rudest form, gave a sanction to the rules of morality, long before the age of artificial reasoning and philosophy. That the terrors of religion should thus enforce the natural sense of duty, was of too much importance to the happiness of mankind for nature to leave it dependent upon the slowness and uncertainty of philosophical researches.

MS 273

The idea that, however we may escape the observation of man or be placed above the reach of human punishment, yet we are always acting under the eye and exposed to the punishment of God, the great avenger of injustice, is a motive capable of restraining the most headstrong passions, with those at least who, by constant reflection, have rendered it familiar to them.

It is in this manner that religion enforces the natural sense of duty . . .

MS 281

Wherever the natural principles of religion are not corrupted by the factious and party zeal of some worthless cabal; wherever the first duty which it requires is to fulfil all the obligations of morality; wherever men are not taught to regard frivolous observances as more immediate duties of religion than acts of justice and beneficence; and to imagine, that by sacrifices, and ceremonies, and vain supplications, they can bargain with the Deity for fraud, and perfidy, and violence, the world undoubtedly judges right in this respect, and justly places a double confidence in the rectitude of the religious man's behaviour.

MS 281, 282

It may be laid down as a certain maxim, that, all other things being supposed equal, the richer the church, the poorer must necessarily be, either the sovereign on the one hand, or the people on the other; and, in all cases, the less able must the state be to defend itself.

WN 765

Where the church benefices are all nearly equal, none of them can be very great, and this mediocrity of benefice, though it may no doubt be carried too far, has, however, some very agreeable effects. Nothing but the most exemplary morals can give dignity to a man of small fortune. The vices of levity and vanity necessarily render him ridiculous, and, are, besides, almost as ruinous to him as they are to the common people. In his own conduct, therefore, he is óbliged to follow that system of morals which the common people respect the most. He gains their esteem and affection by that plan of life which his own interest and situation would lead him to follow.

WN 762

The clergy of an established and well-endowed religion frequently become men of learning and elegance, who can possess all the virtues of gentlemen, or which can recommend them to the esteem of gentlemen; but they are apt gradually to lose the qualities, both good and bad, which gave them authority and influence with the inferior ranks of people, and which had perhaps been the original causes of the success and establishment of their religion.

WN 741

Actions . . . which either produce actual evil, or attempt to produce it, and thereby put us in immediate fear of it, are by the Author of nature rendered the only proper and approved objects of human punishment and resentment. Sentiments, designs, affections, though it is from these that according to cool reason human actions derive their whole merit or demerit, are placed by that great Judge of hearts beyond the limits of every human jurisdiction, and are reserved for the cognizance of his own unerring tribunal.

MS 195

When by natural principles we are led to advance those ends which a refined and enlightened reason would recommend to us, we are very apt to impute to that reason, as to their efficient cause, the sentiments and actions by which we advance those ends, and to imagine that to be the wisdom of man, which in reality is the wisdom of God.

MS 168, 169

The gradual improvements of arts, manufactures, and commerce, the same causes which destroyed the power of the great barons, destroyed in the same manner, through the greater part of Europe, the whole temporal power of the clergy. In the produce of arts, manufactures, and commerce, the clergy, like the great barons, found something for which they could exchange their rude produce, and thereby discovered the means of spending their whole revenues upon their own persons, without giving any considerable share of them to other people. Their charity became gradually less extensive, their hospitality less numerous, and by degrees dwindled away altogether. . . . The inferior ranks of people no longer looked upon that order, as they had done before, as the comforters of their distress, and the relievers of their indigence. On the contrary, they were provoked and disgusted by the vanity, luxury, and expense of the richer clergy, who appeared to spend upon their own pleasures what had always before been regarded as the patrimony of the poor.

WN 755, 756

In little religious sects . . . the morals of the common people have been almost always remarkably regular and orderly; generally much more so than in the established church. The morals of those little sects, indeed, have frequently been rather disagreeably rigorous and unsocial. . . .

Science is the great antidote to the poison of enthusiasm and superstition; and where all the superior ranks of people were secured from it, the inferior ranks could not be much exposed to it.

WN 747, 748

The administration of the great system of the universe, however, the care of the universal happiness of all rational and sensible beings, is the business of God, and not of man. To man is allotted a much humbler department, but one much more suitable to the weakness of his powers, and to the narrowness of his comprehension — the care of his own happiness, of that of his family, his friends, his country: that he is occupied in contemplating the more sublime, can never be an excuse for his neglecting the more humble department.

MS 386

5

Conduct and Morality

In every civilised society, in every society where the distinction of ranks has once been completely established, there have been always two different schemes or systems of morality current at the same time; of which the one may be called the strict or austere; the other the liberal, or, if you will, the loose system. The former is generally admired and revered by the common people: the latter is commonly more esteemed and adopted by what are called people of fashion. The degree of disapprobation with which we ought to mark the vices of levity, the vices which are apt to arise from great prosperity, and from the excess of gaiety and good humour, seems to constitute the principal distinction between those two opposite schemes or systems. In the liberal or loose system, luxury, wanton and even disorderly mirth, the pursuit of pleasure to some degree of intemperance, the breach of chastity, at least in one of the two sexes, etc., provided that they are not accompanied with gross indecency, and do not lead to falsehood or injustice, are generally treated with a good deal of indulgence, and are easily either excused or pardoned altogether. In the austere system, on the contrary, those excesses are regarded with the utmost abhorrence and detestation. The vices of levity are always ruinous to the common people, and a single week's thoughtlessness and dissipation is often sufficient to undo a poor workman for ever, and to drive him through despair upon committing the most enormous crimes. The wiser and better sort of the common people, therefore, have always the utmost abhorrence and detestation of such excesses, which their experience tells them are so immediately fatal to people of their condition. The disorder and extravagance of several years, on the contrary, will not always ruin a man of fashion, and people of that rank are very apt to consider the power of indulging in some degree of excess as one of the advantages of their fortune, and the liberty of doing so without censure or reproach as one of the privileges which belong to their station. In people of their own station, therefore, they regard such excesses with but a small degree of disapprobation, and censure them either very slightly or not at all.

WN 746, 747

The general maxims of morality are formed, like all other general maxims, from experience and induction. We observe, in a great variety of particular cases, what pleases or displeases our moral faculties, what these approve or disapprove of; and by induction from this experience we establish those general rules.

MS 505

In the courts of princes, in the drawing-rooms of the great, where success and preferment depend, not upon the esteem of intelligent and well-informed equals, but upon the fanciful and foolish favour of ignorant, presumptuous, and proud superiors; flattery and falsehood too often prevail over merit and abilities.

MS 129

This disposition to admire, and almost to worship, the rich and the powerful, and to despise or, at least, to neglect, persons of poor and mean condition, though necessary both to establish and to maintain the distinction of ranks and the order of society, is, at the same time, the great and most universal cause of the corruption of our moral sentiments. That wealth and greatness are often regarded with the respect and admiration which are due only to wisdom and virtue; and that the contempt, of which vice and folly are the only proper objects, is often most unjustly bestowed upon poverty and weakness, has been the complaint of moralists in all ages.

MS 126

To deserve, to acquire, and to enjoy, the respect and admiration of mankind, are the great objects of ambition and emulation. Two different roads are presented to us, equally leading to the attainment of this so much desired object; the one, by the study of wisdom and the practice of virtue; the other, by the acquisition of wealth and greatness. Two different characters are presented to our emulation; the one of proud ambition and ostentatious avidity; the other, of humble modesty and equitable justice. . . . The great mob may seem more extraordinary, most frequently the disinterested admirers and worshippers, of wealth and greatness.

MS 126, 127

All for ourselves, and nothing for other people, seems, in every age of the world, to have been the vile maxim of the masters of mankind.

WN 388, 389

The man who, by some sudden revolution of fortune, is lifted up all at once into a condition of life greatly above what he had formerly lived in, may be assured that the congratulations of his best friends are not all of them perfectly sincere. . . . If the chief part of human happiness arises from the consciousness of being beloved, as I believe it does, those sudden changes of fortune seldom contribute much to happiness. He is happiest who advances more gradually to greatness, whom the public destines to every step of his preferment long before he arrives at it, in whom, upon that account, when it comes, it can excite no extravagant joy, and with regard to whom it cannot reasonably create either any jealousy in those he overtakes, or any envy in those he leaves behind.

MS 97, 98

Of all the passions, however, which are so extravagantly disproportioned to the value of their objects, love is the only one that appears, even to the weakest minds, to have any thing in it that is either graceful or agreeable. In itself, first of all, though it may be ridiculous, it is not naturally odious; and though its consequences are often fatal and dreadful, its intentions are seldom mischievous.

MS 85

Love is an agreeable, resentment a disagreeable passion: and accordingly we are not half so anxious that our friends should adopt our friendships, as that they should enter into our resentments.

MS 56

The hasty, fond, and foolish intimacies of young people, founded commonly upon some slight similarity of character altogether unconnected with good conduct, upon a taste, perhaps, for the same studies, the same amusements, the same diversions, or upon their agreement in some singular principle or opinion not commonly adopted; those intimacies which a freak begins, and which a freak puts an end to, how agreeable soever they may appear while they last, can by no means deserve the sacred and venerable name of friendship.

MS 368

Though reason is undoubtedly the source of the general rules of morality, and of all the moral judgments which we form by means of them, it is altogether absurd and unintelligible to suppose that the first perceptions of right and wrong can be derived from reason, even in those particular cases upon the experience of which the general rules are formed. These first perceptions, as well as all other experiments upon which any general rules are founded, cannot be the object of reason, but of immediate sense and feeling. It is by finding, in a vast variety of instances, that one tenor of conduct constantly pleases in a certain manner, and that another as constantly displeases the mind, that we form the general rules of morality. But reason cannot render any particular object either agreeable or disagreeable to the mind for its own sake. Reason may shew that this object is the means of obtaining some other which is naturally either pleasing or displeasing, and in this manner may render it either agreeable or disagreeable, for the sake of something else. But nothing can be agreeable or disagreeable for its own sake, which is not rendered such by immediate sense and feeling. If virtue, therefore, in every particular instance, necessarily pleases for its own sake, and if vice as certainly displeases the mind, it cannot be reason, but immediate sense and feeling, which in this manner reconciles us to the one and alienates us from the other.

MS 506

6

Virtue and Vice

Vice is always capricious — virtue only is regular and orderly.

MS 368

We are angry, for a moment, even at the stone that hurts us. A child beats it, a dog barks at it, a choleric man is apt to curse it. The least reflection, indeed, corrects this sentiment, and we soon become sensible, that what has no feeling is a very improper object of revenge.

MS 178

A woman who paints could derive, one should imagine, but little vanity from the compliments that are paid to her complexion. These, we should expect, ought rather to put her in mind of the sentiments which her real complexion would excite, and mortify her the more by the contrast. To be pleased with such groundless applause is a proof of the most superficial levity and weakness. It is what is properly called vanity, and is the foundation of the most ridiculous and contemptible vices, the vices of affectation and common lying; follies which, if experience did not teach us how common they are, one should imagine the least spark of common sense would save us from.

MS 209, 210

Self-deceit, this fatal weakness of mankind, is the source of half the disorders of human life. If we saw ourselves in the light in which others see us, or in which they would see us if they knew all, a reformation would generally be unavoidable. We could not otherwise endure the sight.

MS 263

The great source of both the misery and disorders of human life seems to arise from overrating the difference between one permanent situation and another. Avarice overrates the difference between poverty and riches: ambition, that between a private and a public station: vainglory, that between obscurity and extensive reputation.

MS 250

Hatred and anger are the greatest poison to the happiness of a good mind.

MS 92

The common proverbial maxims of prudence, being founded in universal experience, are perhaps the best general rules which can be given about it. To affect, however, a very strict and literal adherence to them, would evidently be the most absurd and ridiculous pedantry.

MS 287, 288

Generosity is different from humanity. Those two qualities, which at first sight seem so nearly allied, do not always belong to the same person. Humanity is the virtue of a woman, generosity of a man. The fair sex, who have commonly much more tenderness than ours, have seldom so much generosity. That women rarely make considerable donations is an observation of the civil law. Humanity consists merely in the exquisite fellow-feeling which the spectator entertains with the sentiments of the persons principally concerned, so as to grieve for their sufferings, to resent their injuries, and to rejoice at their good fortune. The most humane actions require no self-denial, no self-command, no great exertion of the sense of propriety. They consist only in doing what this exquisite sympathy would of its own accord prompt us to do. But it is otherwise with generosity. We never are generous except when in some respect we prefer some other person to ourselves, and sacrifice some great and important interest of our own to an equal interest of a friend or of a superior.

MS 313

Beneficence is always free, it cannot be extorted by force, the mere want of it exposes to no punishment; because the mere want of beneficence tends to do no real positive evil. It may disappoint of the good which might reasonably have been expected, and upon that account it may justly excite dislike and disapprobation; it cannot, however, provoke any resentment which mankind will go along with.

MS 155

Nobody but a beggar chooses to depend chiefly upon the benevolence of his fellow-citizens.

WN 14

No benevolent man ever lost altogether the fruits of his benevolence. If he does not always gather them from the persons from whom he ought to have gathered them, he seldom fails to gather them, and with a tenfold increase, from other people. Kindness is the parent of kindness; and if to be beloved by our brethren be the great object of our ambition, the surest way of obtaining it is by our conduct to shew that we really love them.

MS 369

Self-command is not only itself a great virtue, but from it all the other virtues seem to derive their principal lustre.

MS 392

If we examine the different shades and gradations of weakness and self-command, as we meet with them in common life, we shall very easily satisfy ourselves that this control of our passive feelings must be acquired, not from the abstruse syllogisms of a quibbling dialectic, but from that great discipline which Nature has established for the acquisition of this and of every other virtue; a regard to the sentiments of the real or supposed spectator of our conduct.

MS 244

A certain intrepidity, a certain firmness of nerves and hardiness of constitution, whether natural or acquired, are undoubtedly the best preparatives for all the great exertions of self-command.

MS 398

The qualities most useful to ourselves are, first of all, superior reason and understanding, by which we are capable of discerning the remote consequences of all our actions, and of foreseeing the advantage or detriment which is likely to result from them; and, secondly, self-command, by which we are enabled to abstain from present pleasure or to endure present pain, in order to obtain a greater pleasure or to avoid a greater pain in some future time. In the union of those two qualities consists the virtue of prudence, of all the virtues that which is most useful to the individual.

MS 310, 311

The care of the health, of the fortune, of the rank and reputation of the individual, the objects upon which his

comfort and happiness in this life are supposed principally to depend, is considered as the proper business of
that virtue which is commonly called prudence.

MS 349

We talk of the prudence of the great general, of the
great statesman, of the great legislator. Prudence is, in all
these cases, combined with many greater and more
splendid virtues; with valour, with extensive and strong
benevolence, with a sacred regard to the rules of justice,
and all these supported by a proper degree of self-
command. This superior prudence, when carried to the
highest degree of perfection, necessarily supposes the art,
the talent, and the habit or disposition of acting with the
most perfect propriety in every possible circumstance and
situation. It necessarily supposes the utmost perfection of
all the intellectual and of all the moral virtues. It is the
best head joined to the best heart.

MS 353, 354

Humanity does not desire to be great, but to be beloved.

MS 276

Man was made for action, and to promote by the exertion of his faculties such changes in the external circumstances both of himself and others, as may seem most
favourable to the happiness of all. He must not be
satisfied with indolent benevolence, nor fancy himself the

friend of mankind, because in his heart he wishes well to the prosperity of the world. . . . The man who has performed no single action of importance, but whose whole conversation and deportment express the justest, the noblest, and the most generous sentiments, can be entitled to demand no very high reward, even though his inutility should be owing to nothing but the want of an opportunity to serve. We can still refuse it him without blame. We can still ask him, What have you done? What actual service can you produce, to entitle you to so great a recompence? We esteem you and love you; but we owe you nothing.

MS 196

7

Sympathy

To what purpose should we trouble ourselves about the world in the moon?

MS 238

Commiseration for those miseries which we never saw, which we never heard of, but which we may be assured are at all times infesting such numbers of our fellow-creatures, ought, they think, to damp the pleasures of the fortunate, and to render a certain melancholy dejection habitual to all men. . . . This artificial commiseration, besides, is not only absurd, but seems altogether unattainable; and those who affect this character have commonly nothing but a certain affected and sentimental sadness, which, without reaching the heart, serves only to render the countenance and conversation impertinently dismal and disagreeable.

MS 237, 238

When we condole with our friends in their afflictions, how little do we feel in comparison of what they feel? . . . Nature, it seems, when she loaded us with our own sorrows, thought that they were enough, and therefore did not command us to take any further share in those of others, than what was necessary to prompt us to relieve them.

MS 108

We can sympathize with the distress which excessive hunger occasions, when we read the description, of it in the journal of a siege, or of a sea-voyage. We imagine ourselves in the situation of the sufferers, and thence readily conceive the grief, the fear, and consternation, which must necessarily distract them. We feel, ourselves, some degree of those passions, and therefore sympathize with them: but as we do not grow hungry by reading the description, we cannot properly, even in this case, be said to sympathize with their hunger.

It is the same case with the passion by which nature unites the two sexes. Though naturally the most furious of all the passions, all strong expressions of it are upon every occasion indecent, even between persons in whom its most complete indulgence is acknowledged by all laws, both human and divine, to be perfectly innocent. There seems, however, to be some degree of sympathy even with this passion. To talk to a woman as we should to a man is improper: it is expected that their company should inspire us with more gaiety, more pleasantry, and more attention; and an entire insensibility to the fair sex renders a man contemptible in some measure even to the men.

MS 76, 77

A man may sympathize with a woman in child-bed, though it is impossible that he should conceive himself as suffering her pains in his own proper person and character.

MS 502

How selfish soever man may be supposed, there are evidently some principles in his nature, which interest him in the fortune of others, and render their happiness necessary to him, though he derives nothing from it, except the pleasure of seeing it. Of this kind is pity or compassion, the emotion which we feel for the misery of others, when we either see it, or are made to conceive it in a very lively manner. That we often derive sorrow from the sorrow of others, is a matter of fact too obvious to require any instances to prove it; for this sentiment, like all the other original passions of human nature, is by no means confined to the virtuous and humane, though they perhaps may feel it with the most exquisite sensibility. The greatest ruffian, the most hardened violator of the laws of society, is not altogether without it.

MS 47

Pity and compassion are words appropriated to signify our fellow-feeling with the sorrow of others. Sympathy, though its meaning was, perhaps, originally the same, may now, however, without much impropriety, be made use of to denote our fellow-feeling with any passion whatever.

MS 49

It is from this very illusion of the imagination, that the foresight of our own dissolution is so terrible to us, and that the idea of those circumstances, which undoubtedly can give us no pain when we are dead, makes us miserable while we are alive. And from thence arises one of the most important principles in human nature, the dread of death — the great poison to the happiness, but the great restraint upon the injustice of mankind; which, while it afflicts and mortifies the individual, guards and protects the society.

MS 53

Nothing is more graceful than habitual cheerfulness, which is always founded upon a peculiar relish for all the little pleasures which common occurrences afford. We readily sympathize with it; it inspires us with the same joy, and makes every trifle turn up to us in the same agreeable aspect in which it presents itself to the person endowed with this happy disposition.

MS 99

To the selfish and original passions of human nature, the loss or gain of a very small interest of our own appears to be of vastly more importance, excites a much more passionate joy or sorrow, a much more ardent desire or aversion, than the greatest concern of another with whom we have no particular connection. His interests, as long as they are surveyed from his station, can never be put into the balance with our own, can never restrain us from doing whatever may tend to promote our own, how ruinous soever to him. Before we can make any proper comparison of those opposite interests, we must change our position. We must view them, neither from our own place nor yet from his, neither with our own eyes not yet with his, but from the place and with the eyes of a third person, who has no particular connection with either, and who judges with impartiality between us. Here, too, habit and experience have taught us to do this so easily and so readily, that we are scarce sensible that we do it; and it requires, in this case, too, some degree of reflection, and even of philosophy, to convince us, how little interest we should take in the greatest concerns of our neighbour, how little we should be affected by whatever relates to him, if the sense of propriety and justice did not correct the otherwise natural inequality of our sentiments.

MS 233

If we consider all the different passions of human nature, we shall find that they are regarded as decent or indecent, just in proportion as mankind are more or less disposed to sympathize with them.

MS 75

8

The Impartial Spectator

When I endeavour to examine my own conduct, when I endeavour to pass sentence on it, and either to approve or condemn it, it is evident that, in all such cases, I divide myself, as it were, into two persons; and that I, the examiner and judge, represent a different character from that other I, the person whose conduct is examined into and judged of. The first is the spectator, whose sentiments with regard to my own conduct I endeavour to enter into, by placing myself in his situation, and by considering how it would appear to me, when seen from that particular point of view. The second is the agent, the person whom I properly call myself, and of whose conduct, under the character of a spectator, I was endeavouring to form some opinion. The first is the judge; the second the person judged of. But that the judge should, in every respect, be the same with the person

judged of, is as impossible as that the cause should, in
every respect, be the same with the effect.

MS 206, 207

There are two different occasions upon which we
examine our own conduct, and endeavour to view it in the
light in which the impartial spectator would view it: first,
when we are about to act; and, secondly, after we have
acted. Our views are apt to be very partial in both cases;
but they are apt to be most partial when it is of the most
importance that they should be otherwise.

MS 261

The principle by which we naturally either approve or
disapprove of our own conduct, seems to be altogether
the same with that by which we exercise the like judgments concerning the conduct of other people.

MS 203

We suppose ourselves the spectators of our own behaviour, and endeavour to imagine what effect it would,
in this light, produce upon us. This is the only looking-
glass by which we can, in some measure, with the eyes of
other people, scrutinize the propriety of our own conduct.

MS 206

The opinion which we entertain of our own character
depends entirely on our judgment concerning our past
conduct. It is so disagreeable to think ill of ourselves, that

we often purposely turn away our view from those circumstances which might render that judgment unfavourable. He is a bold surgeon, they say, whose hand does not tremble when he performs an operation upon his own person; and he is often equally bold who does not hesitate to pull off the mysterious veil of self-delusion which covers from his view the deformities of his own conduct.

MS 262, 263

Concern for our own happiness recommends to us the virtue of prudence; concern for that of other people, the virtues of justice and beneficence — of which the one restrains us from hurting, the other prompts us to promote that happiness. Independent of any regard either to what are or to what ought to be, or to what upon a certain condition would be the sentiments of other people, the first of those three virtues is originally recommended to us by our selfish, the other two by our benevolent affections.

MS 422

Let us suppose that the great empire of China, with all its myriads of inhabitants, was suddenly swallowed up by an earthquake, and let us consider how a man of humanity in Europe, who had no sort of connection with that part of the world, would be affected upon receiving intelligence of this dreadful calamity. He would, I imagine, first of all express very strongly his sorrow for the misfortune of that unhappy people, he would make many melancholy reflections upon the precariousness of human life, and the vanity of all the labours of man, which could thus be annihilated in a moment. He would, too, perhaps, if he was a man of speculation, enter into many reasonings concerning the effects which this disaster might produce upon the commerce of Europe, and the trade and business of the world in general. And when all this fine philosophy was over, when all these humane sentiments had been once fairly expressed, he would pursue his business or his pleasure, take his repose or his diversion, with the same ease and tranquillity as if no such accident had happened. The most frivolous disaster which could befall himself would occasion a more real disturbance. If he was to lose his little finger to morrow, he would not sleep to-night; but, provided he never saw them, he will snore with the most profound security over the ruin of a hundred millions of his brethren, and the destruction of that immense multitude seems plainly an object less interesting to him than this paltry misfortune of his own. To prevent, therefore, this paltry misfortune to himself, would a man of humanity be willing to sacrifice the lives of a hundred millions of his brethren, provided he had never seen them? Human nature startles with horror at the thought, and the world, in its greatest depravity and corruption, never produced such a villain as could be capable of entertaining it. But what makes this difference? when our passive feelings are almost always so sordid and so selfish, how comes it that our active principles should often be so generous and so noble? When we are always

so much more deeply affected by whatever concerns ourselves than by whatever concerns other men; what is it
which prompts the generous upon all occasions, and the
mean upon many, to sacrifice their own interests to the
greater interests of others? It is not the soft power of
humanity, it is not that feeble spark of benevolence which
Nature has lighted up in the human heart, that is thus
capable of counteracting the strongest impulses of self-
love. It is a stronger power, a more forcible motive,
which exerts itself upon such occasions. It is reason,
principle, conscience, the inhabitant of the breast, the
man within, the great judge and arbiter of our conduct. It
is he who, whenever we are about to act so as to affect the
happiness of others, calls to us, with a voice capable of
astonishing the most presumptuous of our passions, that
we are but one of the multitude, in no respect better than
any other in it; and that when we prefer ourselves so
shamefully and so blindly to others, we become the
proper objects of resentment, abhorrence, and execration.
It is from him only that we learn the real littleness of
ourselves, and of whatever relates to ourselves, and the
natural misrepresentations of self-love can be corrected
only by the eye of this impartial spectator. It is he who
shews us the propriety of generosity and the deformity of
injustice; the propriety of resigning the greatest interests
of our own for the yet greater interests of others; and the
deformity of doing the smallest injury to another in order
to obtain the greatest benefit to ourselves. It is not the
love of our neighbour, it is not the love of mankind,

which upon many occasions prompts us to the practice of those divine virtues. It is a stronger love, a more powerful affection, which generally takes place upon such occasions; the love of what is honourable and noble, of the grandeur, and dignity, and superiority of our own characters.

MS 233, 234, 235

The insolence and brutality of anger, in the same manner, when we indulge its fury without check or restraint, is, of all objects, the most detestable.

MS 71

The man of real constancy and firmness, the wise and just man who has been thoroughly bred in the great school of self-command, in the bustle and business of the world, exposed, perhaps, to the violence and injustice of faction, and to the hardships and hazards of war, maintains this control of his passive feelings upon all occasions; and whether in solitude or in society, wears nearly the same countenance, and is affected very nearly in the same manner. In success and in disappointment, in prosperity and in adversity, before friends and before enemies, he has often been under the necessity of supporting this manhood. He has never dared to forget for one moment the judgment which the impartial spectator would pass upon his sentiments and conduct. He has never dared to suffer the man within the breast to be absent one moment from his attention. With the eyes of this great inmate he has always been accustomed to regard whatever relates to himself. This habit has become perfectly familiar to him: he has been in the constant practice, and, indeed, under the constant necessity, of modelling, or of endeavouring to model, not only his outward conduct and behaviour, but, as much as he can, even his inward sentiments and feelings, according to those of this awful and respectable judge. He does not merely affect the sentiments of the impartial spectator; he really adopts them. He almost identifies himself with, he almost becomes himself that impartial spectator, and scarce even feels but as that great arbiter of his conduct directs him to feel.

MS 246, 247

The propriety of our moral sentiments is never so apt to be corrupted as when the indulgent and partial spectator is at hand, while the indifferent and impartial one is at a great distance.

MS 257

Every man is, no doubt, by nature, first and principally recommended to his own care; and as he is fitter to take care of himself, than of any other person, it is fit and right that it should be so. . . . If he would act so as that the impartial spectator may enter into the principles of his conduct, which is what of all things he has the greatest desire to do, he must upon this, as upon all other occasions, humble the arrogance of his self-love, and bring it down to something which other men can go along with.

MS 161, 162

9

Self-Interest

In every part of the universe we observe means adjusted with the nicest artifice to the ends which they are intended to produce; and in the mechanism of a plant, or animal body, admire how every thing is contrived for advancing the two great purposes of nature, the support of the individual, and the propagation of the species.

MS 168

As to love our neighbour as we love ourselves is the great law of Christianity, so it is the great precept of nature to love ourselves only as we love our neighbour, or, what comes to the same thing, as our neighbour is capable of loving us.

MS 72

Every man, as the Stoics used to say, is first and principally recommended to his own care; and every man is certainly, in every respect, fitter and abler to take care of himself than of any other person. Every man feels his own pleasures and his own pains more sensibly than those of other people. The former are the original sensations — the latter the reflected or sympathetic images of those sensations. The former may be said to be the substance — the latter the shadow.

MS 359

It is the interest of every man to live as much at his ease as he can; and if his emoluments are to be precisely the same, whether he does or does not perform some very laborious duty, it is certainly his interest, at least as interest is vulgarly understood, either to neglect it altogether, or, if he is subject to some authority which will not suffer him to do this, to perform it in as careless and slovenly a manner as that authority will permit. If he is naturally active and a lover of labour, it is his interest to employ that activity in any way from which he can derive some advantage, rather than in the performance of his duty, from which he can derive none.

WN 718

In this consists the difference between the character of a miser and that of a person of exact economy and assiduity. The one is anxious about small matters for their own sake; the other attends to them only in consequence of the scheme of life which he has laid down to himself.

MS 286

The virtue of frugality lies in a middle between avarice and profusion, of which the one consists in an excess, the other in a defect, of the proper attention to the objects of self-interest.

MS 438

When the happiness or misery of others depends in any respect upon our conduct, we dare not, as self-love might suggest to us, prefer the interests of one to that of many. The man within immediately calls to us, that we value ourselves too much and other people too little, and that, by doing so, we render ourselves the proper object of the contempt and indignation of our brethren. Neither is this sentiment confined to men of extraordinary magnanimity and virtue. It is deeply impressed upon every tolerably good soldier, who feels that he would become the scorn of his companions if he could be supposed capable of shrinking from danger, or of hesitating either to expose or to throw away his life when the good of the service required it.

MS 235, 236

We are delighted to find a person who values us as we value ourselves, and distinguishes us from the rest of mankind, with an attention not unlike that with which we distinguish ourselves.

MS 180

The man who esteems himself as he ought, and no more than he ought, seldom fails to obtain from other people all the esteem that he himself thinks due. He desires no more than is due to him, and he rests upon it with complete satisfaction.

MS 419, 420

Nothing can be more absurd . . . than to imagine that men in general should work less when they work for themselves, than when they work for other people. A poor independent workman will generally be more industrious than even a journeyman who works by the piece. The one enjoys the whole produce of his own industry; the other shares it with his master. The one, in his separate independent state, is less liable to the temptations of bad company, which in large manufactories so frequently ruin the morals of the other. The superiority of the independent workman over those servants who are hired by the month or by the year, and whose wages and maintenance are the same whether they do much or little, is likely to be still greater.

WN 83, 84

No regulation of commerce can increase the quantity of industry in any society beyond what its capital can maintain. It can only divert a part of it into a direction into which it might not otherwise have gone; and it is by no means certain that this artificial direction is likely to be more advantageous to the society than that into which it would have gone of its own accord.

Every individual is continually exerting himself to find

out the most advantageous employment for whatever capital he can command. It is his own advantage, indeed, and not that of the society, which he has in view. But the study of his own advantage naturally, or rather necessarily leads him to prefer that employment which is most advantageous to the society.

WN 421

Man has almost constant occasion for the help of his brethren, and it is in vain for him to expect it from their benevolence only. He will be more likely to prevail if he can interest their self-love in his favour, and show them that it is for their own advantage to do for him what he requires of them. Whoever offers to another a bargain of any kind, proposes to do this. Give me that which I want, and you shall have this which you want, is the meaning of every such offer; and it is in this manner that we obtain from one another the far greater part of those good offices which we stand in need of. It is not from the benevolence of the butcher, the brewer, or the baker that we expect our dinner, but from their regard to their own interest. We address ourselves, not to their humanity but to their self-love, and never talk to them of our own necessities but of their advantages.

WN 14

10

Money, Gold, and Wealth

It would be too ridiculous to go about seriously to prove that wealth does not consist in money, or in gold and silver; but in what money purchases, and is valuable only for purchasing.

WN 406

That wealth consists in money, or in gold and silver, is a popular notion which naturally arises from the double function of money, as the instrument of commerce and as the measure of value. In consequence of its being the instrument of commerce, when we have money we can more readily obtain whatever else we have occasion for than by means of any other commodity. The great affair, we always find, is to get money. When that is obtained, there is no difficulty in making any subsequent purchase.

WN 398

The value of money is in proportion to the quantity of the necessaries of life which it will purchase.

WN 836

It is not for its own sake that men desire money, but for the sake of what they can purchase with it.

WN 407

Upon every account . . . the attention of government never was so unnecessarily employed as when directed to watch over the preservation or increase of the quantity of money in any country.

No complaint, however, is more common than that of a scarcity of money. Money, like wine, must always be scarce with those who have neither wherewithal to buy it nor credit to borrow it. Those who have either will seldom be in want either of the money or of the wine which they have occasion for. This complaint, however, of the scarcity of money is not always confined to improvident spendthrifts. It is sometimes general through a whole mercantile town and the country in its neighborhood. Over-trading is the common cause of it. Sober men, whose projects have been disproportioned to their capitals, are as likely to have neither wherewithal to buy money nor credit to borrow it, as prodigals whose expense has been disproportioned to their revenue. Before their projects can be brought to bear, their stock is gone, and the credit with it. They run about everywhere to borrow money, and everybody tells them that they have none to lend. Even such general complaints of the scarcity of money do not always prove that the usual number of gold and silver pieces are not circulating in the country, but that many people want those pieces who have nothing to give for them. When the profits of trade happen to be greater than ordinary, over-trading becomes a general error both among great and small dealers. They do not always send more money abroad than usual, but they buy upon credit, both at home and abroad, an unusual quantity of goods, which they send to some distant market in hopes that the returns will come in before the demand for payment. The demand comes before the returns, and they have nothing at hand with which they can either purchase money, or give solid security for borrowing. It is not any scarcity of gold and silver, but for the difficulty which such people find in borrowing, and which their creditors find in getting payment, that occasions the general complaint of the scarcity of money.

WN 405, 406

In order to put industry into motion, three things are requisite; materials to work upon, tools to work with, and the wages or recompence for the sake of which the work is done. Money is neither a material to work upon, nor a tool to work with; and though the wages of the workman are commonly paid to him in money, his real revenue, like that of all other men, consists, not in the money, but in the money's worth; not in the metal pieces, but in what can be got for them.

WN 279, 280

The judicious operations of banking, by substituting paper in the room of a great part of this gold and silver, enables the country to convert a great part of this dead stock into active and productive stock; into stock which produces something to the country. The gold and silver money which circulates in any country may very properly be compared to a highway, which, while it circulates and carries to market all the grass and corn of the country, produces itself not a single pile of either. The judicious operations of banking, by providing, if I may be allowed so violent a metaphor, a sort of waggon-way through the air, enable the country to convert, as it were, a great part of its highways into good pastures and corn-fields, and thereby to increase very considerably the annual produce of its land and labour. The commerce and industry of the country, however, it must be acknowledged, though they may be somewhat augmented, cannot be altogether so secure when they are thus, as it were, suspended upon the Daedalian wings of paper money as when they travel about upon the solid ground of gold and silver.

WN 304, 305

The substitution of paper in the room of gold and silver money, replaces a very expensive instrument of commerce with one much less costly, and sometimes equally convenient. Circulation comes to be carried on by a new wheel, which it costs less both to erect and to maintain than the old one. But in what manner this operation is performed, and in what manner it tends to increase either the gross or the neat revenue of the society, is not altogether so obvious, and may therefore require some further explication.

There are several different sorts of paper money; but the circulating notes of banks and bankers are the species which is best known, and which seems best adapted for this purpose.

When the people of any particular country have such confidence in the fortune, probity, and prudence of a particular banker, as to believe that he is always ready to pay upon demand such of his promissory notes as are likely to be at any time presented to him; those notes come to have the same currency as gold and silver money, from the confidence that such money can at any time be had for them.

WN 276, 277

Princes and sovereign states have frequently fancied that they had a temporary interest to diminish the quantity of pure metal contained in their coins; but they seldom have fancied that they had any to augment it. The quantity of metal contained in the coins, I believe, of all nations, has, accordingly, been almost continually diminishing, and hardly ever augmenting.

WN 34

In the course of a century or two, it is possible that new mines may be discovered more fertile than any that have ever yet been known; and it is just equally possible that

the most fertile mine then known may be more barren
than any that was wrought before the discovery of the
mines of America. Whether the one or the other of those
two events may happen to take place is of very little
importance to the real wealth and prosperity of the world,
to the real value of the annual produce of the land and
labour of mankind.

WN 237

It is the great multiplication of the productions of all
the different arts, in consequence of the division of labour,
which occasions, in a well-governed society, that universal opulence which extends itself to the lowest ranks of
the people. Every workman has a great quantity of his
own work to dispose of beyond what he himself has occasion for; and every other workman being exactly in the
same situation, he is enabled to exchange a great quantity
of his own goods for a great quantity, or, what comes to
the same thing, for the price of a great quantity of theirs.
He supplies them abundantly with what they have occasion for, and they accommodate him as amply with what
he has occasion for, and a general plenty diffuses itself
through all the different ranks of the society.

WN 11

When the division of labour has been once thoroughly
established, it is but a very small part of a man's wants
which the produce of his own labour can supply. He
supplies the far greater part of them by exchanging that

surplus part of the produce of his own labour, which is over and above his own consumption, for such parts of the produce of other men's labour as he has occasion for. Every man thus lives by exchanging, or becomes in some measure a merchant, and the society itself grows to be what is properly a commercial society.

WN 22, 23

I thought it necessary, though at the hazard of being tedious, to examine at full length this popular notion that wealth consists in money, or in gold and silver. Money in common language, as I have already observed, frequently signifies wealth, and this ambiguity or expression has rendered this popular notion so familiar to us that even they who are convinced of its absurdity are very apt to forget their own principles, and in the course of their reasonings to take it for granted as a certain and undeniable truth. Some of the best English writers upon commerce set out with observing that the wealth of a country consists, not in its gold and silver only, but in its lands, houses, and consumable goods of all different kinds. In the course of their reasonings, however, the lands, houses, and consumable goods seem to slip out of their memory, and the strain of their argument frequently supposes that all wealth consists in gold and silver, and that to multiply those metals is the great object of national industry and commerce.

WN 417, 418

11

Labour and Wages

The annual labour of every nation is the fund which originally supplies it with all the necessaries and conveniences of life which it annually consumes . . .

WN lvii

The greatest improvement in the productive powers of labour, and the greater part of the skill, dexterity, and judgment with which it is any where directed, or applied, seem to have been the effects of the division of labour.

WN 3

To take an example, therefore, from a very trifling manufacture; but one in which the division of labour has been very often taken notice of, the trade of the pin-maker; a workman not educated to this business (which the division of labour has rendered a distinct trade), nor acquainted with the use of the machinery employed in it (to the invention of which the same division of labour has probably given occasion), could scarce, perhaps, with his utmost industry, make one pin in a day and certainly could not make twenty. But in the way in which this business is now carried on, not only the whole work is a peculiar trade, but it is divided into a number of branches, of which the greater part are likewise peculiar trades. One man draws out the wire, another straightens it, a third cuts it, a fourth points it, a fifth grinds it at the top for receiving the head; to make the head requires two or three distinct operations; to put it on is a peculiar business, to whiten the pins is another; it is even a trade by itself to put them into the paper; and the important business of making a pin is, in this manner, divided into about eighteen distinct operations, which, in some manufactories, are all performed by distinct hands, though in others the same man will sometimes perform two or three of them. I have seen a small manufactory of this kind where ten men only were employed, and where some of them consequently performed two or three distinct operations. But though they were very poor and therefore but indifferently accommodated with the necessary machinery, they could, when they exerted themselves, make among them about twelve pounds of pins in a day. There are in a pound upwards of four thousand pins of a middling size. Those ten persons, therefore, could make among them upwards of forty-eight thousand pins in a day. Each person, therefore, making a tenth part of forty-eight thousand pins, might be considered as making four thousand eight hundred pins in a day. But if they had all wrought separately and independently, and without any of them having been educated to this peculiar business, they certainly could not each of them have made twenty, perhaps not one pin in a day; that is, certainly, not the two hundred and fortieth, perhaps not the four thousand eight hundredth part of what they are at present capable of performing, in consequence of a proper division and combination of their different operations.

WN 4, 5

The division of labour, however, so far as it can be introduced, occasions, in every art, a proportionable increase of the productive powers of labour. The separation of different trades and employments from one another seems to have taken place in consequences of this advantage. This separation, too, is generally carried furthest in those countries which enjoy the highest degree of industry and improvement; what is the work of one man in a rude state of society being generally that of several in an improved one. In every improved society, the farmer is generally nothing but a farmer; the manufacturer, nothing but a manufacturer.

WN 5, 6

This great increase of the quantity of work, which, in consequence of the division of labour, the same number of people are capable of performing, is owing to three different circumstances; first, to the increase of dexterity in every particular workman; secondly, to the saving of the time which is commonly lost in passing from one species of work to another; and lastly, to the invention of a great number of machines which facilitate and abridge labour, and enable one man to do the work of many.

WN 7

Observe the accommodation of the most common artificer or day-labourer in a civilised and thriving country, and you will perceive that the number of people of whose industry a part, though but a small part, has been employed in procuring him this accommodation, exceeds all computation. The woollen coat, for example, which covers the day-labourer, as coarse and rough as it may appear, is the produce of the joint labour of a great multitude of workmen. The shepherd, the sorter of the wool, the wool-comber or carder, the dyer, the scribbler, the spinner, the weaver, the fuller, the dresser, with many others, must all join their different arts in order to complete even this homely production. How many merchants and carriers, besides, must have been employed in transporting the materials from some of those workmen to others who often live in a very distant part of the country! How much commerce and navigation in particular, how many ship-builders, sailors, sail-makers, rope-makers, must have been employed in order to bring together the different drugs made use of by the dyer, which often come from the remotest corners of the world! What a

variety of labour, too, is necessary in order to produce the
tools of the meanest of those workmen! To say nothing of
such complicated machines as the ship of the sailor, the
mill of the fuller, or even the loom of the weaver, let us
consider only what a variety of labour is requisite in order
to form that very simple machine, the shears with which
the shepherd clips the wool. The miner, the builder of the
furnace for smelting the ore, the seller of the timber, the
burner of the charcoal to be made use of in the smelting-
house, the brick-maker, the brick-layer, the workmen
who attend the furnace, the mill-wright, the forger, the
smith, must all of them join their different arts in order to
produce them. Were we to examine, in the same manner,
all the different parts of his dress and household furniture,
the coarse linen shirt which he wears next to his skin, the
shoes which cover his feet, the bed which he lies on, and
all the different parts which compose it, the kitchen-grate
at which he prepares his victuals, the coals which he
makes use of for that purpose, dug from the bowels of the
earth, and brought to him perhaps by a long sea and a
long land carriage, all the other utensils of his kitchen, all
the furniture of his table, the knives and forks, the earthen
or pewter plates upon which he serves up and divides his
victuals, the different hands employed in preparing his
bread and his beer, the glass window which lets in the
heat and the light, and keeps out the wind and the rain,
with all the knowledge and art requisite for preparing that
beautiful and happy invention, without which these
northern parts of the world could scarce have afforded a

very comfortable habitation, together with the tools of all the different workmen employed in producing those different conveniences; if we examine, I say, all these things, and consider what a variety of labour is employed about each of them, we shall be sensible that, without the assistance and co-operation of many thousands, the very meanest person in a civilised country could not be provided, even according to what we very falsely imagine the easy and simple manner in which he is commonly accommodated. Compared, indeed, with the more extravagant luxury of the great, his accommodation must no doubt appear extremely simple and easy; and yet it may be true, perhaps, that the accommodation of a European prince does not always so much exceed that of an industrious and frugal peasant as the accommodation of the latter exceeds that of many an African king, the absolute master of the lives and liberties of ten thousand naked savages.

WN 11, 12

This division of labour, from which so many advantages are derived, is not originally the effect of any human wisdom, which foresees and intends that general opulence to which it gives occasion. It is the necessary, though very slow and gradual consequence of a certain propensity in human nature which has in view no such extensive utility; the propensity to truck, barter, and exchange one thing for another.

WN 13

The invention of all those machines by which labour is so much facilitated and abridged seems to have been originally owing to the division of labour. Men are much more likely to discover easier and readier methods of attaining any object when the whole attention of their minds is directed towards that single object than when it is dissipated among a great variety of things. But in consequence of the division of labour, the whole of every man's attention comes naturally to be directed towards some one very simple object. It is naturally to be expected, therefore, that some one or other of those who are employed in each particular branch of labour should soon find out easier and readier methods of performing their own particular work, wherever the nature of it admits of such improvement. A great part of the machines made use of in those manufactures in which labour is most subdivided, were originally the inventions of common workmen, who, being each of them employed in some very simple operation, naturally turned their thoughts towards finding out easier and readier methods of performing it.

WN 9, 10

It appears, accordingly, from the experience of all ages and nations, I believe, that the work done by freemen comes cheaper in the end than that performed by slaves. . . .

The liberal reward of labour, therefore, as it is the effect of increasing wealth, so it is the cause of increasing

population. To complain of it is to lament over the necessary effect and cause of the greatest public prosperity.

WN 80, 81

The liberal reward of labour, as it encourages the propagation, so it increases the industry of the common
people. The wages of labour are the encouragement of
industry, which, like every other human quality, improves in proportion to the encouragement it receives. A
plentiful subsistence increases the bodily strength of the
labourer, and the comfortable hope of bettering his condition, and of ending his days perhaps in ease and plenty,
animates him to exert that strength to the utmost. Where
wages are high, accordingly, we shall always find the
workmen more active, diligent, and expeditious, than
where they are low.

WN 81

As it is the power of exchanging that gives occasion to
the division of labour, so the extent of this division must
always be limited by the extent of that power, or, in other
words, by the extent of the market. When the market is
very small, no person can have any encouragement to
dedicate himself entirely to one employment, for want of
the power to exchange all that surplus part of the produce
of his own labour, which is over and above his own
consumption, for such parts of the produce of other men's
labour as he has occasion for.

WN 17, 18

A man grows rich by employing a multitude of manufacturers: he grows poor by maintaining a multitude of
menial servants. . . . The wages of labour vary with the
ease or hardship, the cleanliness or dirtiness, the honour-
ableness or dishonourableness of the employment. . . .
Honour makes a great part of the reward of all honourable
professions.

WN 100

Labour, like commodities, may be said to have a real
and a nominal price. Its real price may be said to consist in
the quantity of the necessaries and conveniences of life
which are given for it; its nominal price, in the quantity of
money. The labourer is rich or poor, is well or ill re-
warded, in proportion to the real, not to the nominal price
of his labour.

WN 33

When in any country the demand for those who live by
wages, labourers, journeymen, servants of every kind, is
continually increasing; when every year furnishes
employment for a greater number than had been
employed the year before, the workmen have no occasion
to combine in order to raise their wages. The scarcity of
hands occasions a competition among masters, who bid
against one another, in order to get workmen, and thus
voluntarily break through the natural combination of masters not to raise wages.

WN 68

It is not the actual greatness of national wealth, but its continual increase, which occasions a rise in the wages of labour. It is not, accordingly, in the richest countries, but in the most thriving, or in those which are growing rich the fastest, that the wages of labour are highest.

WN 69

The price of labour, it must be observed, cannot be ascertained very accurately anywhere, different prices being often paid at the same place and for the same sort of labour, not only according to the different abilities of the workmen, but according to the easiness or hardness of the masters. Where wages are not regulated by law, all that we can pretend to determine is what are the most usual; and experience seems to show that law can never regulate them properly, though it has often pretended to do so.

WN 77, 78

Whenever the law has attempted to regulate the wages of workmen, it has always been rather to lower them than to raise them.

WN 131

The property which every man has in his own labour, as it is the original foundation of all other property, so it is the most sacred and inviolable. The patrimony of a poor man lies in the strength and dexterity of his hands; and to hinder him from employing this strength and dexterity in what manner he thinks proper without injury to his neighbour is a plain violation of this most sacred property. It is a manifest encroachment upon the just liberty both of the workman and of those who might be disposed to employ him. As it hinders the one from working at what he thinks proper, so it hinders the others from employing whom they think proper. To judge whether he is fit to be employed may surely be trusted to the discretion of the employers whose interest it so much concerns. The affected anxiety of the law-giver lest they should employ an improper person is evidently as impertinent as it is oppressive.

WN 121, 122

The whole of the advantages and disadvantages of the different employments of labour and stock must, in the same neighbourhood, be either perfectly equal or continually tending to equality. If in the same neighbourhood, there was any employment evidently either more or less advantageous than the rest, so many people would crowd into it in the one case, and so many would desert it in the other, that its advantages would soon return to the level of other employments. This at least would be the case in a society where things were left to follow their natural course, where there was perfect liberty, and where every man was perfectly free both to choose what occupation he thought proper, and to change it as often as he thought proper. Every man's interest would prompt him to seek the advantageous, and to shun the disadvantageous employment.

WN 99

12

Capital and Profit

In that rude state of society in which there is no division of labour, in which exchanges are seldom made, and in which every man provides everything for himself, it is not necessary that any stock should be accumulated or stored up beforehand in order to carry on the business of the socity. . . .

But when the division of labour has once been thoroughly introduced, the produce of a man's own labour can supply but a very small part of his occasional wants. The far greater part of them are supplied by the produce of other men's labour, which he purchases with the produce, or, what is the same thing, with the price of the produce of his own. But this purchase cannot be made till such time as the produce of his own labour has not only been completed, but sold. A stock of goods of different kinds, therefore, must be stored up somewhere sufficient to maintain him, and to supply him with the materials and tools of his work till such time, at least, as both these events can be brought about. A weaver cannot apply himself entirely to his peculiar business unless there is beforehand stored up somewhere, either in his own possession or in that of some other person, a stock sufficient to maintain him, and to supply him with the materials and tools of his work, till he has not only completed, but sold his web. The accumulation must, evidently, be previous to his applying his industry for so long a time to such a peculiar business.

WN 259

As the accumulation of stock must, in the nature of things, be previous to the division of labour, so labour can be more and more subdivided in proportion only as stock is previously more and more accumulated. The quantity of materials which the same number of people can work up, increases in a great proportion as labour comes to be more and more subdivided; and as the operations of each workman are gradually reduced to a greater degree of simplicity, a variety of new machines come to be invented for facilitating and abridging those operations. As the division of labour advances, therefore, in order to give constant employment to an equal number of workmen, an equal stock of provisions, and a greater stock of materials and tools than what would have been necessary in a ruder state of things, must be accumulated beforehand. But the number of workmen in every branch of business generally increases with the division of labour in that branch, or rather it is the increase of their number which enables them to class and subdivide themselves in this manner.

WN 260

As the accumulation of stock is previously necessary for carrying on this great improvement in the productive powers of labour, so that accumulation naturally leads to this improvement. The person who employs his stock in maintaining labour, necessarily wishes to employ it in such a manner as to produce as great a quantity of work as possible. He endeavours, therefore, both to make among his workmen the most proper distribution of employment, and to furnish them with the best machines which he can either invent or afford to purchase. His abilities in both these respects are generally in proportion to the extent of his stock, or to the number of people whom it can employ. The quantity of industry, therefore, not only increases in every country with the increase of the stock which employs it, but, in consequence of that increase, the same quantity of industry produces a much greater quantity of work.

Such are in general the effects of the increase of stock upon industry and its productive powers

WN 260

Traders and other undertakers may, no doubt, with great propriety, carry on a very considerable part of their

projects with borrowed money. In justice to their creditors, however, their own capital ought, in this case, to be
sufficient to ensure, if I may say so, the capital of those
creditors; or to render it extremely improbable that those
creditors should incur any loss, even though the success
of the project should fall very much short of the expectation of the projectors. Even with this precaution too, the
money which is borrowed, and which it is meant should
not be repaid till after a period of several years, ought not
to be borrowed of a bank, but ought to be borrowed upon
bond or mortgage, of such private people as propose to
live upon the interest of their money, without taking the
trouble themselves to employ the capital; and who are
upon that account willing to lend that capital to such
people of good credit as are likely to keep it for several
years. A bank, indeed, which lends its money without the
expense of stampt paper, or of attornies' fees for drawing
bonds and mortgages, and which accepts of repayment
upon the easy terms of the banking companies of Scotland; would, no doubt, be a very convenient creditor to
such traders and undertakers. But such traders and undertakers would, surely, be most inconvenient debtors to
such a bank.

WN 291, 292

The lowest ordinary rate of interest must, in the same
manner, be something more than sufficient to compensate
the occasional losses to which lending, even with toler-

able prudence, is exposed. Were it not more, charity or friendship could be the only motives for lending.

WN 96

The prejudices of some political writers against shop-keepers and tradesmen are altogether without foundation. So far is it from being necessary either to tax them or to restrict their numbers that they can never be multiplied so as to hurt the public, though they may so as to hurt one another. The quantity of grocery goods, for example, which can be sold in a particular town is limited by the demand of that town and its neighbourhood. The capital, therefore, which can be employed in the grocery trade cannot exceed what is sufficient to purchase that quantity. If this capital is divided between two different grocers, their competition will tend to make both of them sell cheaper than if it were in the hands of one only; and if it were divided among twenty, their competition would be just so much the greater, and the chance of their combining together, in order to raise the price, just so much the less. Their competition might perhaps ruin some of them-selves; but to take care of this is the business of the parties concerned, and it may safely be trusted to their discretion. It can never hurt either the consumer or the producer; on the contrary, it must tend to make the retailers both sell cheaper and buy dearer than if the whole trade was monopolised by one or two persons. Some of them, perhaps, may sometimes decoy a weak customer to buy what he has no occasion for. This evil, however, is of too little importance to deserve the public attention, nor would it necessarily be prevented by restricting their numbers. It is not the multitude of ale-houses, to give the most suspicious example, that occasions a general disposition to drunkenness among the common people; but that disposition arising from other causes necessarily gives employment to a multitude of ale-houses.

WN 342, 343

In all countries where there is tolerable security, every man of common understanding will endeavour to employ whatever stock he can command in procuring either present enjoyment or future profit. If it is employed in procuring present enjoyment, it is a stock reserved for immediate consumption. If it is employed in procuring future profit, it must procure this profit either by staying with him, or by going from him. In the one case it is a fixed, in the other it is a circulating capital. A man must be perfectly crazy who, where there is tolerable security, does not employ all the stock which he commands, whether it be his own or borrowed of other people, in some one or other of those three ways.

WN 268

The profits of stock, it may perhaps be thought, are only a different name for the wages of a particular sort of labour, the labour of inspection and direction. They are, however, altogether different, are regulated by quite different principles, and bear no proportion to the quantity, the hardship, or the ingenuity of this supposed labour of inspection and direction. They are regulated altogether by the value of the stock employed, and are greater or smaller in proportion to the extent of this stock.

This original state of things, in which the labourer enjoyed the whole produce of his own labour, could not last beyond the first introduction of the appropriation of land and the accumulation of stock. It was at an end, therefore, long before the most condiserable improvements were made in the productive powers of labour, and it would be to no purpose to trace further what might have been its effects upon the recompense or wages of labour.

As soon as land becomes private property, the landlord demands a share of almost all the produce which the labourer can either raise, or collect from it. His rent makes the first deduction from the produce of the labour which is employed upon land.

It seldom happens that the person who tills the ground has wherewithal to maintain himself till he reaps the harvest. His maintenance is generally advanced to him from the stock of a master, the farmer who employs him, and who would have no interest to employ him, unless he was to share in the produce of his labour, or unless his stock was to be replaced to him with a profit. This profit makes a second deduction from the produce of the labour which is employed upon land.

The produce of almost all other labour is liable to the

like deduction of profit. In all arts and manufactures the greater part of the workmen stand in need of a master to advance them the materials of their work, and their wages and maintenance till it be completed. He shares in the produce of their labour, or in the value which it adds to the materials upon which it is bestowed; and in this share consists his profit.

WN 65

The rise and fall in the profits of stock depend upon the same causes with the rise and fall in the wages of labour, the increasing or declining state of the wealth of the society.

WN 87

Profit is so very fluctuating that the person who carries on a particular trade cannot always tell you himself what is the average of his annual profit. . . . To ascertain what is the average profit of all the different trades carried on in a great kingdom must be a much more difficult; and to judge of what it may have been formerly, or in remote periods of time, with any degree of precision, must be altogether impossible.

WN 87

When profit diminishes, merchants are very apt to complain that trade decays; though the diminution of profit is the natural effect of its prosperity, or of a greater stock being employed in it than before.

WN 91

A merchant, it has been said very properly, is not necessarily the citizen of any particular country. It is in a great measure indifferent to him from what place he carries on his trade; and a very trifling disgust will make him remove his capital, and together with it all the industry which it supports, from one country to another. No part of it can be said to belong to any particular country, till it has been spread as it were over the face of that country, either in buildings, or in the lasting improvement of lands.

WN 395

In raising the price of commodities the rise of wages operates in the same manner as simple interest does in the accumulation of debt. The rise of profit operates like compound interest. Our merchants and master-manufacturers complain much of the bad effects of high wages in raising the price, and thereby lessening the sale of their goods both at home and abroad. They say nothing concerning the bad effects of high profits. They are silent with regard to the pernicious effects of their own gains. They complain only of those of other people.

WN 98

The keeper of an inn or tavern, who is never master of his own house, and who is exposed to the brutality of every drunkard, exercises neither a very agreeable nor a very creditable business. But there is scarce any common trade in which a small stock yields so great a profit.

WN 101

Capitals are increased by parsimony, and diminished by prodigality and misconduct.

WN 321

Whatever a person saves from his revenue he adds to his capital, and either employs it himself in maintaining an additional number of productive hands, or enables some other person to do so, by lending it to him for an interest, that is, for a share of the profits. As the capital of an individual can be increased only by what he saves from his annual revenue or his annual gains, so the capital of a society, which is the same with that of all the individuals who compose it, can be increased only in the same manner.

WN 321

Parsimony, and not industry, is the immediate cause of the increase of capital. Industry, indeed, provides the subject which parsimony accumulates. But whatever industry might acquire, if parsimony did not save and store up, the capital would never be the greater.

WN 321

A great stock, though with small profits, generally increases faster than a small stock with great profits. Money, says the proverb, makes money. When you have got a little, it is often easy to get more. The great difficulty is to get that little.

WN 93

13

Land and Rent

The lands of no country, it is evident, can ever be completely cultivated and improved till once the price of every produce, which human industry is obliged to raise upon them, has got so high as to pay for the expense of complete improvement and cultivation. In order to do this, the price of each particular produce must be sufficient, first, to pay the rent of good corn land, as it is that which regulates the rent of the greater part of other cultivated land; and, secondly, to pay the labour and expense of the farmer as well as they are commonly paid upon good corn land; or, in other words, to replace with the ordinary profits the stock which he employs about it.

WN 227, 228

When by the improvement and cultivation of land the labour of one family can provide food for two, the labour of half the society becomes sufficient to provide food for the whole. The other half, therefore, or at least the greater part of them, can be employed in providing other things, or in satisfying the other wants and fancies of mankind. Clothing and lodging, household furniture, and what is called Equipage, are the principal objects of the greater part of those wants and fancies. The rich man consumes no more food than his poor neighbour. In quality it may be very different, and to select and prepare it may require more labour and art; but in quantity it is very nearly the same. But compare the spacious palace and great wardrobe of the one with the hovel and the few rags of the other, and you will be sensible that the difference between their clothing, lodging, and household furniture is almost as great in quantity as it is in quality. The desire of food is limited in every man by the narrow capacity of the human stomach; but equipage, and household furniture, seems to have no limit or certain boundary. Those, therefore, who have the command of more food than they themselves can consume, are always willing to exchange the surplus, or, what is the same thing, the price of it, for gratifications of this other kind. What is over and above satisfying the limited desire is given for the amusement of those desires which cannot be satisfied, but seem to be altogether endless. The poor, in order to obtain food, exert themselves to gratify those fancies of the rich, and to obtain it more certainly they vie with one another in the cheapness and perfection of their work. The number of workmen increases with the increasing quantity of food, or with the growing improvement and cultivation of the lands; and as the nature of their business admits of the utmost subdivisions of labour, the quantity of materials which they can work up increases in a much greater proportion than their numbers. Hence arises a demand for every sort of material which human invention can employ, either usefully or ornamentally, in building, dress, equipage, or household furniture; for the fossils and minerals contained in the bowels of the earth; the precious metals, and the precious stones.

WN 163, 164

As soon as the land of any country has all become private property, the landlords, like all other men, love to reap where they never sowed, and demand a rent even for its natural produce. The wood of the forest, the grass of the field, and all the natural fruits of the earth, which, when land was in common, cost the labourer only the trouble of gathering them, come, even to him, to have an additional price fixed upon them. He must then pay for the license to gather them; and must give up to the landlord a portion of what his labour either collects or produces. This portion, or, what comes to the same thing, the price of this portion, constitutes the rent of land, and in the price of the greater part of commodites makes a third component part.

WN 49

The rent of land, it may be thought, is frequently no more than a reasonable profit or interest for the stock laid out by the landlord upon its improvement. This, no doubt, may be partly the case upon some occasions; for it can scarce ever be more than partly the case. The landlord demands a rent even for unimproved land, and the supposed interest or profit upon the expense of improvement is generally an addition to this original rent.

WN 144, 145

The rent of land, therefore, is considered as the price paid for the use of the land, is naturally a monopoly price. It is not at all proportioned to what the landlord may have laid out upon the improvement on the land, or to what he can take; but to what the farmer can afford to give.

WN 145

All those improvements in the productive powers of labour, which tend directly to reduce the real price of manufactures, tend indirectly to raise the real rent of land. The landlord exchanges that part of his rude produce, which is over and above his own consumption, or what comes to the same thing, the price of that part of it, for manufactured produce. Whatever reduces the real price of the latter, raises that of the former. An equal quantity of the former becomes thereby equivalent to a greater quantity of the latter; and the landlord is enabled to purchase a greater quantity of the conveniences, ornaments, or luxuries, which he has occasion for.

WN 248

Every increase in the real wealth of the society, every increase in the quantity of useful labour employed within it, tends indirectly to raise the real rent of land.

WN 248

Rent, it is to be observed, therefore, enters into the composition of the price of commodities in a different way from wages and profit. High or low wages and profit are the causes of high or low price; high or low rent is the effect of it. It is because high or low wages and profit must be paid, in order to bring a particular commodity to market, that its price is high or low. But it is because its price is high or low; a great deal more, or very little more, or no more, than what is sufficient to pay those wages and profit, that it affords a high rent, or a low rent, or no rent at all.

WN 145, 146

In general, there is not, perhaps, any one article of expense or consumption by which the liberality or narrowness of a man's whole expense can be better judged of, than by his house-rent.

WN 794

In country houses, at a distance from any great town, where there is plenty of ground to choose upon, the ground rent is scarce any thing, or no more than what the ground which the house stands upon would pay if employed in agriculture. In country villas in the neighbourhood of some great town, it is sometimes a good deal higher; and the peculiar conveniency or beauty of situation is there frequently very well paid for. Ground rents are generally highest in the capital, and in those particular parts of it where there happens to be the greatest demand for houses, whatever be the business, for pleasure and society, or for mere vanity and fashion.

WN 791, 792

It does not, perhaps, relate to the present subject, but I cannot help remarking it, that very old families, such as have possessed some considerable estate from father to son for many successive generations are very rare in commercial countries. In countries which have little commerce, on the contrary, such as Wales or the highlands of Scotland, they are very common.

WN 391, 392

Laws frequently continue in force long after the circumstances which first gave occasion to them, and which could alone render them reasonable, are no more.

WN 361, 362

Lands, for the purposes of pleasure and magnificence, parks, gardens, public walks, &c. possessions which are every where considered as causes of expense, not as sources of revenue, seem to be the only lands which, in a great and civilized monarchy, ought to belong to the crown.

WN 776

If the rod be bent too much one way, says the proverb, in order to make it straight you must bend it as much the other. The French philosophers, who have proposed the system which represents agriculture as the sole source of the revenue and wealth of every country, seem to have adopted this proverbial maxim; and as in the plan of Mr. Colbert the industry of the towns was certainly over-valued in comparison with that of the country; so in their system it seems to be as certainly undervalued.

WN 628

This system [the Physiocratic system] . . . with all its imperfections is, perhaps, the nearest approximation to the truth that has yet been published upon the subject of political economy, and is upon that account well worth the consideration of every man who wishes to examine with attention the principles of that very important science. Though in representing the labour which is employed upon land as the only productive labour, the notions which it inculcates are perhaps too narrow and confined; yet in representing the wealth of nations as consisting, not in the unconsumable riches of money, but in the consumable goods annually reproduced by the labour of the society, and in representing perfect liberty as the only effectual expedient for rendering this annual reproduction the greatest possible, its doctrine seems to be in every respect as just as it is generous and liberal.

WN 642

14

The Market and Prices

Nobody ever saw one animal by its gestures and natural cries signify to another, this is mine, that yours: I am willing to give this for that.

WN 13

The word value, it is to be observed, has two different meanings, and sometimes expresses the utility of some particular object, and sometimes the power of purchasing other goods which the possession of that objective conveys. The one may be called "value in use;" the other, "value in exchange." The things which have the greatest value in use have frequently little or no value in exchange; and, on the contrary, those which have the greatest value in exchange have frequently little or no value in use. Nothing is more useful than water: but it will purchase scarce anything; scarce anything can be had in exchange for it. A diamond, on the contrary, has scarce any value in use; but a very great quantity of other goods may frequently be had in exchange for it.

WN 28

At all times and places that is dear which it is difficult to come at, or which it costs much labour to acquire; and that cheap which is to be had easily, or with very little labour. Labour alone, therefore, never varying in its own value, is alone the ultimate and real standard by which the value of all commodities can at all times and places be estimated and compared. It is their real price; money is their nominal price only.

WN 33

The real value of all the different component parts of price, it must be observed, is measured by the quantity of labour which they can, each of them, purchase or command. Labour measures the value not only of that part of price which resolves itself into labour, but of that which resolves itself into rent, and of that which resolves itself into profit.

WN 50

The real price of everything, what everything really costs to the man who wants to acquire it, is the toil and trouble of acquiring it.

WN 30

In that early and rude state of society which precedes both the accumulation of stock and the appropriation of land, the proportion between the quantities of labour necessary for acquiring different objects seems to be the only circumstance which can afford any rule for exchanging them for one another. If among a nation of hunters, for example, it usually costs twice the labour to kill a beaver which it does to kill a deer, one beaver should naturally exchange for or be worth two deer. It is natural that what is usually the produce of two days' or two hours' labour, should be worth double of what is usually the produce of one day's or one hour's labour.

WN 47

What everything is really worth to the man who has acquired it, and who wants to dispose of it or exchange it for something else, is the toil and trouble which it can save to himself, and which it can impose upon other people. What is bought with money or with goods is purchased by labour as much as what we acquire by the toil of our own body. That money or those goods indeed save us this toil. They contain the value of a certain quantity of labour which we exchange for what is supposed at the time to contain the value of an equal quantity. Labour was the first price, the original purchase-money that was paid for all things. It was not by gold or by silver, but by labour, that all the wealth of the world was originally purchased; and its value, to those who possess it, and who want to exchange it for some new productions, is precisely equal to the quantity of labour which it can enable them to purchase or command.

Wealth, as Mr. Hobbes says, is power. But the person who either acquires, or succeeds to a great fortune, does not necessarily acquire or succeed to any political power, either civil or military. His fortune may, perhaps, afford him the means of acquiring both, but the mere possession of that fortune does not necessarily convey to him either. The power which that possession immediately and directly conveys to him, is the power of purchasing; a certain command over all the labour, or over all the produce of labour, which is then in the market. His fortune is greater or less, precisely in proportion to the extent of this power; or to the quantity either of other men's labour, or, what is the same thing, of the produce of other men's labour, which it enables him to purchase or command. The exchangeable value of everything must always be precisely equal to the extent of this power which it conveys to its owner.

But though labour be the real measure of the exchangeable value of all commodities, it is not that by which their value is commonly estimated. It is often difficult to ascertain the proportion between two different quantities of labour. The time spent in two different sorts of work will not always alone determine this proportion. The different degrees of hardship endured, and of ingenuity exercised, must likewise be taken into account. There may be more labour in an hour's hard work than in two hours' easy business; or in an hour's application to a trade which it cost ten years' labour to learn, than in a month's industry at an ordinary and obvious employment. But it is not easy to find any accurate measure either of hardship or ingenuity. In exchanging, indeed, the different productions of different sorts of labour for one another, some allowance is commonly made for both. It is adjusted, however, not by any accurate measure, but by the higgling and bargaining of the market, according to that sort of rough equality which, though not exact, is sufficient for carrying on the business of common life.

WN 30, 31

When the price of any commodity is neither more nor less than what is sufficient to pay the rent of the land, the wages of the labour, and the profits of the stock employed in raising, preparing, and bringing it to market, according to their natural rates, the commodity is then sold for what may be called its natural price.

The commodity is then sold precisely for what it is worth, or for what it really costs the person who brings it to market; for though in common language what is called the prime cost of any commodity does not comprehend the profit of the person who is to sell it again, yet if he sell it at a price which does not allow him the ordinary rate of profit in his neighbourhood, he is evidently a loser by the trade; since by employing his stock in some other way he might have made that profit. His profit, besides, is his revenue, the proper fund of his subsistence. As, while he is preparing and bringing the goods to market, he advances to his workmen their wages, or their subsistence; so he advances himself, in the same manner, his own subsistence, which is generally suitable to the profit which he may reasonably expect from the sale of his goods. Unless they yield him this profit, therefore, they do not repay him what they may very properly he said to have really cost him.

Though the price, therefore, which leaves him this profit is not always the lowest at which a dealer may sometimes sell his goods, it is the lowest at which he is likely to sell them for any considerable time; at least where there is perfect liberty, or where he may change his trade as often as he pleases.

WN 55, 56

The actual price at which any commodity is commonly sold is called its market price. It may either be above, or below, or exactly the same with its natural price.

WN 56

When the quantity of any commodity which is brought to market falls short of the effectual demand, all those who are willing to pay the whole value of the rent, wages, and profit, which must be paid in order to bring it thither, cannot be supplied with the quantity which they want. Rather than want it altogether, some of them will be willing to give more. A competition will immediately begin among them, and the market price will rise more or less above the natural price, according as either the greatness of the deficiency, or the wealth and wanton luxury of the competitors, happen to animate more or less the eagerness of the competition.

WN 56

When the quantity brought to market exceeds the effectual demand, it cannot be all sold to those who are willing to pay the whole value of the rent, wages, and profit, which must be paid in order to bring it thither. Some part must be sold to those who are willing to pay less, and the low price which they give for it must reduce the price of the whole. The market price will sink more or less below the natural price, according as the greatness of the excess increases more or less the competition of the sellers, or according as it happens to be more or less important to them to get immediately rid of the commodity. The same excess in the importation of perishable, will contain a much greater competition than in that of durable commodities; in the importation of oranges, for example, than in that of old iron.

WN 57

When the quantity brought to market is just sufficient to supply the effectual demand, and no more, the market price naturally comes to be either exactly, or as nearly as can be judged of, the same with the natural price. The whole quantity upon hand can be disposed of for this price, and cannot be disposed of for more. The competition of the different dealers obliges them all to accept of this price, but does not oblige them to accept of less.

The quantity of every commodity brought to market naturally suits itself to the effectual demand. It is of the interest of all those who employ their land, labour, or stock, in bringing any commodity to market, that the quantity never should exceed the effectual demand; and it is the interest of all other people that it never should fall short of that demand.

WN 57

The natural price, therefore, is, as it were, the central price, to which the prices of all commodities are continually gravitating. Different accidents may sometimes keep them suspended a good deal above it, and sometimes force them down even somewhat below it. But whatever may be the obstacles which hinder them from settling in this center of repose and continuance, they are constantly tending towards it.

The whole quantity of industry annually employed in order to bring any commodity to market, naturally suits itself in this manner to the effectual demand. It naturally aims at bringing always that precise quantity thither which may be sufficient to supply, and no more than supply, that demand.

WN 58

Though the market price of every particular commodity is in this manner continually gravitating, if one may say so, towards the natural price, yet sometimes particular accidents, sometimes natural causes, and sometimes particular regulations of police, may, in many com-

modities keep up the market price, for a long time together, a good deal above the natural price.

WN 59

A monopoly granted either to an individual or to a
trading company has the same effect as a secret in trade or
manufactures. The monopolists, by keeping the market
constantly under-stocked, by never fully supplying the
effectual demand, sell their commodities much above the
natural price, and raise their emoluments, whether they
consist in wages or profit, greatly above their natural rate.

The price of monopoly is upon every occasion the
highest which can be got. The natural price, or the price
of free competition, on the contrary, is the lowest which
can be taken, not upon every occasion, indeed, but for
any considerable time together. The one is upon every
occasion the highest which can be squeezed out of the
buyers, or which, it is supposed, they will consent to
give: the other is the lowest which the sellers can commonly afford to take, and at the same time continue
their business.

The exclusive privileges of corporations, statutes of
apprenticeship, and all those laws which restrain, in particular employments, the competition to a smaller number
than might otherwise go into them, have the same tendency, though in a less degree. They are a sort of enlarged
monopolies, and may frequently, for ages together, and
in whole classes of employments, keep up the market
price of particular commodities above the natural price,
and maintain both the wages of the labour and the profits

of the stock employed about them somewhat above their natural rate.

Such enhancements of the market price may last as long as the regulations of police which give occasion to them.

WN 61, 62

The interest of the inland dealer, and that of the great body of the people, how opposite soever they may at first sight appear, are, even in years of the greatest scarcity, exactly the same. It is his interest to raise the price of his corn as high as the real scarcity of the season requires, and it can never be his interest to raise it higher. By raising the price he discourages the consumption so much that the supply of the season is likely to go beyond the consumption of the season, and to last for some time after the next crop begins to come in, he runs the hazard, not only of losing a considerable part of his corn by natural causes, but of being obliged to sell what remains of it for much less than what he might have had for it several months before. If by not raising the price high enough he discourages the consumption so little that the supply of the season is likely to fall short of the consumption of the season, he not only loses a part of the profit which he might otherwise have made, but he exposes the people to suffer before the end of the season, instead of the hardships of a dearth, the dreadful horrors of a famine. It is the interest of the people that their daily, weekly, and monthly consumption should be proportioned as exactly as possible to the supply of the season. The interest of the inland corn dealer is the same.

WN 490, 491

A country that has no mines of its own must undoubtedly draw its gold and silver from foreign countries in the same manner as one that has no vineyards of its own must draw its wines. It does not seem necessary, however, that the attention of government should be more turned towards the one than towards the other object. A country that has wherewithal to buy wine will never be in want of those metals. They are to be bought for a certain price like all other commodities, and as they are the price of all other commodities, so all other commodities are the price of those metals. We trust with perfect security that the freedom of trade, without any attention of government, will always supply us with the wine which we have occasion for; and we may trust with equal security that it will always supply us with all the gold and silver which we can afford to purchase or to employ, either in circulating our commodities, or in other uses.

The quantity of every commodity which human industry can either purchase or produce naturally regulates itself in every country according to the effectual demand, or according to the demand of those who are willing to pay the whole rent, labour, and profits which must be paid in order to prepare and bring it to market. But no commodities regulate themselves more easily or more exactly according to this effectual demand than gold and silver.

WN 403, 404

15

An Invisible Hand

As every individual . . . endeavours as much as he can both to employ his capital in the support of domestic industry, and so to direct that industry that its produce may be of the greatest value; every individual necessarily labours to render the annual revenue of the society as great as he can. He generally, indeed, neither intends to promote the public interest, nor knows how much he is promoting it. By preferring the support of domestic to that of foreign industry, he intends only his own security; and by directing that industry in such a manner as its produce may be of the greatest value, he intends only his own gain, and he is in this, as in many other cases, led by an invisible hand to promote an end which was no part of his intention. Nor is it always the worse for the society that it was no part of it. By pursuing his own interest he frequently promotes that of the society more effectually than when he really intends to promote it. I have never known much good done by those who affected to trade for the public good.

WN 423

The pleasures of wealth and greatness, when considered in this complex view, strike the imagination as something grand, and beautiful, and noble, of which the attainment is well worth all the toil and anxiety which we are so apt to bestow upon it.

And it is well that nature imposes upon us in this manner. It is this deception which rouses and keeps in continual motion the industry of mankind. It is this which first prompted them to cultivate the ground, to build houses, to found cities and commonwealths, and to invent and improve all the sciences and arts, which ennoble and embellish human life; which have entirely changed the whole face of the globe, have turned the rude forests of nature into agreeable and fertile plains, and made the trackless and barren ocean a new fund of subsistence, and the great high road of communication to the different nations of the earth. The earth, by these labours of mankind, has been obliged to redouble her natural fertility, and to maintain a greater multitude of inhabitants. It is to no purpose that the proud and unfeeling landlord views his extensive fields, and without a thought for the wants of his brethren, in imagination consumes himself the whole harvest that grows upon them. The homely and vulgar proverb, that the eye is larger than the belly, never was more fully verified than with regard to him. The capacity of his stomach bears no proportion to the immensity of his desires, and will receive no more than that of the meanest peasant. The rest he is obliged to distribute among those who prepare, in the nicest manner, that little which he himself makes use of, among those who fit up the palace in which this little is to be consumed, among those who provide and keep in order all the different baubles and trinkets which are employed in the economy of greatness; all of whom thus derive from his luxury and caprice that share of the necessaries of life which they would in vain have expected from his humanity or his justice. The produce of the soil maintains at all times nearly that number of inhabitants which it is capable of maintaining. The rich only select from the heap what is most precious and agreeable. They consume little more than the poor; and in spite of their natural selfishness and rapacity, though they mean only their own conveniency, though the sole end which they propose from the labours of all the thousands whom they employ be the gratification of their own vain and insatiable desires, they divide with the poor the produce of all their improvements. They are led by an invisible hand to make nearly the same distribution of the necessaries of life which would have been made had the earth been divided into equal portions among all its inhabitants; and thus, without intending it, without knowing it, advance the interest of the society, and afford means to the multiplication of the species. When providence divided the earth among a few lordly masters, it neither forgot nor abandoned those who seemed to have been left out in the partition. These last, too, enjoy their share of all that it produces. In what constitutes the real happiness of human life, they are in no respect inferior to those who would seem so much above them. In ease of body and peace of mind, all the different ranks of life are nearly upon a level, and the beggar, who suns himself by the side of the highway, possesses that security which kings are fighting for.

MS 303, 304, 305

But though man is thus employed to alter that distribution of things which natural events would make, if left to themselves; though like the gods of the poets he is perpetually interposing, by extraordinary means, in favour of virtue and in opposition to vice, and, like them, endeavours to turn away the arrow that is aimed at the head of the righteous, but to accelerate the sword of destruction that is lifted up against the wicked; yet he is by no means able to render the fortune of either quite suitable to his own sentiments and wishes. The natural course of things cannot be entirely controlled by the impotent endeavours of man: the current is too rapid and too strong for him to stop it; and though the rules which direct it appear to have been established for the wisest and best purposes, they sometimes produce effects which shock all his natural sentiments. That a great combination of men should prevail over a small one, that those who engage in an enterprise with forethought and all necessary preparation, should prevail over such as oppose them without any; and that every end should be acquired by those means only which nature has established for acquiring it, seems to be a rule not only necessary and unavoidable in itself, but even useful and proper for rousing the industry and attention of mankind.

MS 279

16

Monopoly and Free Trade

In general, if any branch of trade, or any division of labour, be advantageous to the public, the freer and more general the competition, it will always be the more so.

WN 313

Country gentlemen and farmers are, to their great honour, of all people, the least subject to the wretched spirit of monopoly.

WN 428, 429

Country gentlemen and farmers, dispersed in different parts of the country, cannot so easily combine as merchants and manufacturers, who, being collected into towns, and accustomed to that exclusive corporation spirit which prevails in them, naturally endeavour to obtain against all their countrymen the same exclusive privilege which they generally possess against the inhabitants of their respective towns. They accordingly seem to have been the original inventors of those restraints upon the importation of foreign goods which secure to them the monopoly of the home market. It was probably in imitation of them, and to put themselves upon a level with those who, they found, were disposed to oppress them, that the country gentlemen and farmers of Great Britain so far forgot the generosity which is natural to their station as to demand the exclusive privilege of supplying their countrymen with corn and butcher's meat. They did not perhaps take time to consider how much less their interest could be affected by the freedom of trade than that of the people whose example they followed.

To prohibit by a perpetual law the importation of foreign corn and cattle is in reality to enact that the population and industry of the country shall at no time exceed what the rude produce of its own soil can maintain.

WN 429

People of the same trade seldom meet together, even for merriment and diversion, but the conversation ends in a conspiracy against the public, or in some contrivance to raise prices. It is impossible indeed to prevent such meetings, by any law which either could be executed, or would be consistent with liberty and justice. But though the law cannot hinder people of the same trade from sometimes assembling together, it ought to do nothing to facilitate such assemblies, much less to render them necessary.

WN 128

Corporation laws enable the inhabitants of towns to raise their prices, without fearing to be under-sold by the free competition of their own countrymen. Those other regulations secure them equally against that of foreigners. The enhancement of price occasioned by both is everywhere finally paid by the landlords, farmers, and labourers of the country, who have seldom opposed the establishment of such monopolies. They have commonly neither inclination nor fitness to enter into combinations: and the clamour and sophistry of merchants and manufacturers easily persuade them that the private interest of a part, and of a subordinate part of the society, is the general interest of the whole.

WN 127, 128

Good roads, canals, and navigable rivers, by diminishing the expense of carriage, put the remote parts of the country more nearly upon a level with those in the neighbourhood of the town. They are upon that account the greatest of all improvements. They encourage the cultivation of the remote, which must always be the most extensive circle of the country. They are advantageous to the town, by breaking down the monopoly of the country in its neighbourhood. . . .

WN 147, 148

The pretence that corporations are necessary for the
better government of the trade is without any foundation.
The real and effectual discipline which is exercised over a
workman is not that of his corporation, but that of his
customers. It is the fear of losing their employment which
restrains his frauds and corrects his negligence. An exclusive corporation necessarily weakens the force of this
discipline. A particular set of workmen must then be
employed, let them behave well or ill. It is upon this
account that in many large incorporated towns no tolerable workmen are to be found, even in some of the most
necessary trades. If you would have your work tolerably
executed, it must be done in the suburbs, where the
workmen, having no exclusive privilege, have nothing
but their character to depend upon, and you must then
smuggle it into the town as well as you can.

WN 129

Consumption is the sole end and purpose of all production; and the interest of the producer ought to be attended
to, only so far as it may be necessary for promoting that
of the consumer. The maxim is so perfectly self-evident,
that it would be absurd to attempt to prove it. But in the
mercantile system, the interest of the consumer is almost
constantly sacrificed to that of the producer; and it seems
to consider production, and not consumption, as the ultimate end and object of all industry and commerce.

WN 625

Monopoly of one kind or another, indeed, seems to be the sole engine of the mercantile system.

WN 595

The high duties which have been imposed upon the importation of many different sorts of foreign goods, in order to discourage their consumption in Great Britain, have in many cases served only to encourage smuggling; and in all cases have reduced the revenue of the customs below what more moderate duties would have afforded. The saying of Dr. Swift, that in the arithmetic of the customs two and two, instead of making four, make sometimes only one, holds perfectly true with regard to such heavy duties, which never could have been imposed, had not the mercantile system taught us, in many cases, to employ taxation as an instrument, not of revenue, but of monopoly.

WN 832, 833

The case in which it may sometimes be a matter of deliberation how far it is proper to continue the free importation of certain foreign goods, is, when some foreign nation restrains by high duties or prohibitions the importation of some of our manufactures into their country. Revenge in this case naturally dictates retaliation, and that we should impose the like duties and prohibitions upon the importation of some or all of their manufactures into ours. Nations accordingly seldom fail to retaliate in this manner. The French have been particularly forward to favour their own manufactures by restraining the importation of such foreign goods as could come into competition with them. In this consisted a great part of the policy of Mr. Colbert, who, notwithstanding his great abilities, seems in this case to have been imposed upon by the sophistry of merchants and manufacturers, who are always demanding a monopoly against their countrymen.

WN 434

The case in which it may sometimes be a matter of deliberation, how far, or in what manner, it is proper to restore the free importation of foreign goods, after it has been for some time interrupted, is, when particular manufactures, by means of high duties or prohibitions upon all foreign goods which can come into competition with them, have been so far extended as to employ a great multitude of hands. Humanity may in this case require that the freedom of trade should be restored only by slow gradations, and with a good deal of reserve and circumspection. Were those high duties and prohibitions taken away all at once, cheaper foreign goods of the same kind might be poured so fast into the home market, as to deprive all at once many thousands of our people of their ordinary employment and means of subsistence. The disorder which this would occasion might no doubt be very considerable.

WN 435, 436

The wealth of a neighbouring nation, however, though dangerous in war and politics, is certainly advantageous in trade. In a state of hostility it may enable our enemies to maintain fleets and armies superior to our own; but in a state of peace and commerce it must likewise enable them to exchange with us to a greater value, and to afford a better market, either for the immediate produce of our own industry, or for whatever is purchased with that produce. As a rich man is likely to be a better customer to the industrious people in his neighbourhood, than a poor, so is likewise a rich nation. . . . Private people who want to make a fortune, never think of retiring to the remote and poor provinces of the country, but resort either to the capital, or to some of the great commercial towns. They know, that, where little wealth circulates, there is little to be got, but that where a great deal is in motion, some share of it may fall to them. The same maxims which would in this manner direct the common sense of one, or ten or twenty millions, should regulate the judgment of one, or ten, or twenty millions, and should make a whole nation regard the riches of its neighbours, as a probable cause and occasion for itself to acquire riches. A nation that would enrich itself by foreign trade, is certainly most likely to do so when its neighbours are all rich, industrious, and commercial nations.

WN 461, 462

All the original sources of revenue, the wages of labour, the rent of land, and the profits of stock, the monopoly renders much less abundant than they otherwise would be. To promote the little interest of one little order of men in one country, it hurts the interest of all other orders of men in that country, and of all men in all other countries.

WN 578

It is a losing trade, it is said, which a workman carries on with the alehouse; and the trade which a manufacturing nation would naturally carry on with a wine country may be considered as a trade of the same nature. I answer, that the trade with the alehouse is not necessarily a losing trade. In its own nature it is just as advantageous as any other, though perhaps somewhat more liable to be abused. The employment of a brewer, and even that of a retailer of fermented liquors, are as necessary divisions of labour as any other. It will generally be more advantageous for a workman to buy of the brewer the quantity he has occasion for than to brew it himself, and if he is a poor workman, it will generally be more advantageous for him to buy it by little and little of the retailer than a large quantity of the brewer. He may no doubt buy too much of either, as he may of any other dealers in his neighbourhood, of the butcher, if he is a glutton, or of the draper, if he affects to be a beau among his companions. It is advantageous to the great body of workmen, notwithstanding, that all these trades should be free, though this freedom may be abused in all of them, and is more likely to be so, perhaps, in some than in others. Though individuals, besides, may sometimes ruin their fortunes by an excessive consumption of fermented liquors, there seems to be no risk that a nation should do so. Though in every country there are many people who spend upon such liquors more than they can afford, there are always many more who spend less. . . . The Portuguese, it is said, indeed, are better customers for our manufactures than the French, and should therefore be encouraged in preference to them. As they give us their custom, it is pretended, we should give them ours. The sneaking arts of underling tradesmen are thus erected into political maxims for the conduct of a great empire: for it is the most underling tradesmen only who make it a rule to employ chiefly their own customers. A great trader purchases his goods always where they are cheapest and best, without regard to any little interest of this kind.

WN 456, 460

The single advantage which the monopoly procures to a single order of men is in many different ways hurtful to the general interest of the country.

WN 579

Nations have been taught that their interest consisted in beggaring all their neighbours. Each nation has been made to look with an invidious eye upon the prosperity of all the nations with which it trades, and to consider their gain as its own loss. Commerce, which ought naturally to be, among nations, as among individuals, a bond of union and friendship, has become the most fertile source of discord and animosity. The capricious ambition of kinds and ministers has not, during the present and the preceding century, been more fatal to the repose of Europe than the impertinent jealousy of merchants and manufacturers. The violence and injustice of the rulers of mankind is an ancient evil, for which, I am afraid, the nature of human affairs can scarce admit of a remedy. But the mean rapacity, the monopolising spirit of merchants and manufacturers, who neither are, nor ought to be the rulers of mankind, though it cannot perhaps be corrected may very easily be prevented from disturbing the tranquility of anybody but themselves.

That it was the spirit of monopoly which originally both invented and propagated this doctrine cannot be doubted; and they who first taught it were by no means such fools as they who believed in it.

WN 460, 461

In every country it always is and must be the interest of the great body of the people to buy whatever they want of those who sell it cheapest. The proposition is so very manifest that it seems ridiculous to take any pains to prove it; nor could it ever have been called in question had not the interested sophistry of merchants and manufacturers confounded the common sense of mankind. Their interest is, in this respect, directly opposite to that of the great body of the people. As it is the interest of the freemen of a corporation to hinder the rest of the inhabitants from employing any workmen but themselves, so it is the interest of the merchants and manufacturers of every country to secure to themselves the monopoly of the home market.

WN 461

There seem . . . to be two cases in which it will generally be advantageous to lay some burden upon foreign for the encouragement of domestic industry.

The first is, when some particular sort of industry is necessary for the defence of the country. The defence of Great Britain, for example, depends very much upon the number of its sailors and shipping. The act of navigation, therefore, very properly endeavours to give the sailors and shipping of Great Britain the monopoly of the trade of their own country, in some cases by absolute prohibitions and in others by heavy burdens upon the shipping of foreign countries. . . .

The second case, in which it will generally be advantageous to lay some burden upon foreign for the encouragement of domestic industry is, when some tax is imposed at home upon the produce of the latter. In this case, it seems reasonable that an equal tax should be imposed upon the like produce of the former. This would not give the monopoly of the home market to domestic industry, nor turn towards a particular employment a greater share of the stock and labour of the country than what would naturally go to it. It would only hinder any part of what would naturally go to it from being turned away by the tax into a less natural direction, and would leave the competition between foreign and domestic industry, after the tax, as nearly as possible upon the same footing as before it.

WN 429–432

The natural advantages which one country has over another in producing particular commodities are sometimes so great that it is acknowledged by all the world to be in vain to struggle with them. By means of glasses, hotbeds, and hot walls, very good grapes can be raised in Scotland, and very good wine too can be made of them at about thirty times the expense for which at least equally good can be brought from foreign countries. Would it be a reasonable law to prohibit the importation of all foreign wines merely to encourage the making of claret and burgundy in Scotland? But if there would be a manifest absurdity in turning towards any employment thirty times more of the capital and industry of the country than would be necessary to purchase from foreign countries an equal quantity of the commodities wanted, there must be an absurdity, though not altogether so glaring, yet exactly of the same kind, in turning towards any such employment a thirtieth, or even a three-hundredth part more of either.

WN 425, 426

The interest of a nation in its commercial relations to foreign nations is, like that of a merchant with regard to the different people with whom he deals, to buy as cheap and to sell as dear as possible. But it will be most likely to buy cheap, when by the most perfect freedom of trade it encourages all nations to bring to it the goods which it has occasion to purchase; and, for the same reason, it will be most likely to sell dear, when its markets are thus filled with the greatest numbers of buyers.

WN 431

To expect, indeed, that the freedom of trade should ever be entirely restored in Great Britain, is as absurd as to expect that an Oceana or Utopia should ever be established in it. Not only the prejudices of the public, but what is much more unconquerable, the private interests of many individuals, irresistibly oppose it. Were the officers of the army to oppose with the same zeal and unanimity any reduction in the number of forces, with which master manufacturers set themselves against every law that is likely to increase the number of their rivals in the home market; were the former to animate their soldiers, in the same manner as the latter enflame their workmen, to attack with violence and outrage the proposers of any such regulation; to attempt to reduce the army would be as dangerous as it has now become to attempt to diminish in any respect the monopoly which our manufacturers have obtained against us. This monopoly has so much increased the number of some particular tribes of them, that, like an overgrown standing army, they have become formidable to the government, and upon many occasions intimidate the legislature. The member of parliament who supports every proposal for strengthening this monopoly, is sure to acquire not only the reputation of understanding trade, but great popularity and influence with an order of men whose numbers and wealth render them of great importance. If he opposes them, on the contrary, and still more if he has authority enough to be able to thwart them, neither the most acknowledged probity, nor the highest rank, nor the greatest public services, can protect him from the most infamous abuse and detraction, from personal insults, nor sometimes from real danger, arising from the insolent outrage of furious and disappointed monopolists.

WN 437, 438

17

Taxation

E very different order of citizens is bound to contribute
to the support of the sovereign or commonwealth.

WN 618

Before I enter upon the examination of particular taxes,
it is necessary to premise the four following maxims with
regard to taxes in general.

I. The subjects of every state ought to contribute towards the support of the government, as nearly as possible, in proportion to their respective abilities; that is, in
proportion to the revenue which they respectively enjoy
under the protection of the state. The expense of government to the individuals of a great nation is like the expense of management to the joint tenants of a great estate,
who are all obliged to contribute in proportion to their
respective interests in the estate. In the observation or

neglect of this maxim consists what is called the equality or inequality of taxation . . .

II. The tax which each individual is bound to pay ought to be certain, and not arbitrary. The time of payment, the manner of payment, the quantity to be paid, ought all to be clear and plain to the contributor, and to every other person. Where it is otherwise, every person subject to the tax is put more or less in the power of the tax-gatherer, who can either aggravate the tax upon any obnoxious contributor, or extort, by the terror of such aggravation, some present or perquisite to himself. The uncertainty of taxation encourages the insolence and favours the corruption of an order of men who are naturally unpopular, even where they are neither insolent nor corrupt. The certainty of what each individual ought to pay is, in taxation, a matter of so great importance that a very considerable degree of inequality, it appears, I believe, from the experience of all nations, is not near so great an evil as a very small degree of uncertainty.

III. Every tax ought to be levied at the time, or in the manner, in which it is most likely to be convenient for the contributor to pay it. A tax upon the rent of land or of houses, payable at the same term at which such rents are usually paid, is levied at the time when it is most likely to be convenient for the contributor to pay; or, when he is most likely to have wherewithal to pay. Taxes upon such consumable goods as are articles of luxury, are all finally paid by the consumer, and generally in a manner that is very convenient for him. He pays them by little and little, and he has occasion to buy the goods. As he is at liberty, too, either to buy, or not to buy, as he pleases, it must be his own fault if he ever suffers any considerable inconvenience from such taxes.

IV. Every tax ought to be so contrived as both to take out and to keep out of the pockets of the people as little as possible over and above what it brings into the public treasury of the state. A tax may either take out or keep out of the pockets of the people a great deal more than it brings into the public treasury, in the four following ways. First, the levying of it may require a great number of officers, whose salaries may eat up the greater part of the produce of the tax, and whose perquisites may impose another additional tax upon the people. Secondly, it may obstruct the industry of the people, and discourage them from applying to certain branches of business which might give maintenance and employment to great multitudes. While it obliges the people to pay, it may thus diminish, or perhaps destroy, some of the funds which might enable them more easily to do so. Thirdly, by the forfeitures and other penalties which those unfortunate individuals incur who attempt unsuccessfully to evade the tax, it may frequently ruin them, and thereby put an end to the benefit which the community might have received from the employment of their capitals. . . . Fourthly, by subjecting the people to the frequent visits and the odious examination of the tax-gatherers, it may expose them to much unnecessary trouble, vexation, and oppression; and though vexation is not, strictly speaking, expense, it is certainly equivalent to the expense at which every man would be willing to redeem himself from it. It is in some one or other of these four different ways that taxes are frequently so much more burdensome to the people than they are beneficial to the sovereign.

WN 777–779

If direct taxes upon the wages of labour have not always occasioned a proportionable rise in those wages, it is because they have generally occasioned a considerable fall in the demand for labour. The declension of industry, the decrease of employment for the poor, the diminution of the annual produce of the land and labour of the country, have generally been the effects of such taxes. In consequence of them, however, the price of labour must always be higher than it otherwise would have been in the actual state of the demand: and this enhancement of price, together with the profit of those who advance it, must always be finally paid by the landlords and consumers.

WN 817

It is thus that a tax upon the necessaries of life, operates exactly in the same manner as a direct tax upon the wages of labour. The labourer, though he may pay it out of his hand, cannot, for any considerable time at least, be properly said even to advance it. It must always in the long-run be advanced to him by his immediate employer in the advanced rate of his wages. His employer, if he is a manufacturer, will charge upon the price of his goods this rise of wages, together with a profit; so that the final payment of the tax, together with this over-charge, will fall upon the consumer.

WN 822, 823

Taxes upon luxuries have no tendency to raise the price of any other commodities except that of the commodities taxed. Taxes upon necessaries, by raising the wages of labour, necessarily tend to raise the price of all manufactures, and consequently to diminish the extent of their sale and consumption. Taxes upon luxuries are finally paid by the consumers of the commodities taxed, without any retribution. They fall indifferently upon every species of revenue, the wages of labour, the profits of stock, and the rent of land. Taxes upon necessaries, so far as they affect the labouring poor, are finally paid, partly by landlords in the diminished rent of their lands, and partly by rich consumers, whether landlords or others, in the advanced price of manufactured goods; and always with a considerable over-charge. The advanced price of such manufactures as are real necessaries of life, and are destined for the consumption of the poor, or coarse woollens, for example, must be compensated to the poor by a farther advancement of their wages. The middling and superior ranks of people, if they understood their own interest, ought always to oppose all taxes upon the necessaries of life, as well as all direct taxes upon the wages of labour.

WN 824

It does not seem necessary that the expense of those public works should be defrayed from that public revenue, as it is commonly called, of which the collection and application are in most countries assigned to the executive power. The greater part of such public works may easily be so managed, as to afford a particular revenue sufficient for defraying their own expense, without bringing any burden upon the general revenue of the society.

A highway, a bridge, a navigable canal, for example, may in most cases be both made and maintained by a small toll upon the carriages which make use of them: a harbour, by a moderate port-duty upon the tunnage of the shipping which load or unload in it.

WN 682

High taxes, sometimes by diminishing the consumption of the taxed commodities, and sometimes by encouraging smuggling, frequently afford a smaller revenue to government than what might be drawn from more moderate taxes.

WN 835

An injudicious tax offers a great temptation to smuggling. But the penalties of smuggling must rise in proportion to the temptation. The law, contrary to all the ordinary principles of justice, first creates the temptation, and then punishes those who yield to it; and it commonly enhances the punishment, too, in proportion to the very circumstance which ought certainly to alleviate it, the temptation to commit the crime.

WN 779

The ordinary expense of the greater part of modern governments in time of peace being equal or nearly equal to their ordinary revenue, when war comes they are both unwilling and unable to increase their revenue in proportion to the increase of their expense. They are unwilling for fear of offending the people, who, by so great and so sudden an increase of taxes, would soon be disgusted with the war; and they are unable from not well knowing what taxes would be sufficient to produce the revenue wanted. The facility of borrowing delivers them from the embarrassment which this fear and inability would otherwise occasion. By means of borrowing they are enabled, with a very moderate increase of taxes, to raise, from year to year, money sufficient for carrying on the war, and by the practice of perpetually funding they are enabled, with the smallest possible increase of taxes, to raise annually the largest possible sum of money. In great empires the people who live in the capital, and in the provinces remote from the scene of action, feel, many of them, scarce any inconvenience from the war; but enjoy, at their ease, the amusement of reading in the newspapers the exploits of their own fleets and armies. To them this amusement compensates the small difference between the taxes which they pay on account of the war, and those which they had been accustomed to pay in time of peace. They are commonly dissatisfied with the return of peace, which puts an end to their amusement, and to a thousand visionary hopes of conquest and national glory from a longer continuance of the war.

The return of peace, indeed, seldom relieves them from the greater part of the taxes imposed during the war. These are mortgaged for the interest of the debt contracted in order to carry it on. If, over and above paying the interest of this debt, and defraying the ordinary expense of government, the old revenue, together with the new taxes, produce some surplus revenue, it may perhaps be converted into a sinking fund for paying off the debt. But, in the first place, this sinking fund, even supposing it should be applied to no other purpose, is generally altogether inadequate for paying, in the course of any period during which it can reasonably be expected that peace should continue, the whole debt contracted during the war; and, in the second place, this fund is almost always applied to other purposes.

WN 872, 873

Like an improvident spendthrift, whose pressing occasions will not allow him to wait for the regular payment of his revenue, the state is in the constant practice of borrowing of its own factors and agents and of paying interest for the use of its own money.

WN 865

It ought to be remembered, that when the wisest government has exhausted all the proper subjects of taxation, it must, in cases of urgent necessity, have recourse to improper ones.

WN 881

The proprietor of land is necessarily a citizen of the particular country in which his estate lies. The proprietor of stock is properly a citizen of the world, and is not necessarily attached to any particular country. He would be apt to abandon the country in which he was exposed to a vexatious inquisition, in order to be assessed to a burdensome tax, and would remove his stock to some other country where he could either carry on his business, or enjoy his fortune more at his ease. By removing his stock he would put an end to all the industry which it had maintained in the country which he left. Stock cultivates land; stock employs labour. A tax which tended to drive away stock from any particular country, would so far tend to dry up every source of revenue, both to the sovereign and to the society. Not only the profits of stock, but the rent of land and the wages of labour, would necessarily be more or less diminished by its removal.

WN 800

Every tax, however, is to the person who pays it a badge, not of slavery, but of liberty. It denotes that he is subject to government, indeed, but that, as he has some property, he cannot himself be the property of a master.

WN 808

18

Colonies

Empires, like all the other works of men, have all hitherto proved mortal, yet every empire aims at immortality.

WN 781, 782

The discovery of America, and that of a passage to the East Indies by the Cape of Good Hope, are the two greatest and most important events recorded in the history of mankind. Their consequences have already been very great; but, in the short period of between two and three centuries which has elapsed since these discoveries were made, it is impossible that the whole extent of their consequences can have been seen. What benefits or what misfortunes to mankind may hereafter result from those great events, no human wisdom can foresee.

WN 590

Frequently a man of great, sometimes even a man of small fortune, is willing to purchase a thousand pounds share in India stock, merely for the influence which he expects to acquire by a vote in the court of proprietors. It gives him a share, though not in the plunder, yet in the appointment of the plunderers of India; the court of directors, though they make that appointment, being necessarily more or less under the influence of the proprietors, who not only elect those directors, but sometimes overrule the appointments of their servants in India. Provided he can enjoy this influence for a few years, and thereby provide for a certain number of his friends, he frequently cares little about the dividend; or even about the value of the stock upon which his vote is founded. About the prosperity of the great empire, in the government of which that vote gives him a share, he seldom cares at all. No other sovereigns ever were, or, from the nature of things, ever could be, so perfectly indifferent about the happiness or misery of their subjects, the improvements or waste of their dominions, the glory or disgrace of their administration; as, from irresistible moral causes, the greater part of the proprietors of such a mercantile company are, and necessarily must be.

WN 710

Some nations have given up the whole commerce of their colonies to an exclusive company, of whom the colonies were obliged to buy all such European goods as they wanted, and to whom they were obliged to sell the whole of their own surplus produce. It was the interest of the company, therefore, not only to sell the former as dear, and to buy the latter as cheap as possible, but to buy no more of the latter, even at this low price, than what they could dispose of for a very high price in Europe. It was their interest, not only to degrade in all cases the value of the surplus produce of the colony, but in many cases to discourage and keep down the natural increase of its quantity. Of all the expedients that can well be contrived to stunt the natural growth of a new colony, that of an exclusive company is undoubtedly the most effectual.

WN 542

To found a great empire for the sole purpose of raising up a people of customers may at first sight appear a project fit only for a nation of shopkeepers. It is, however, a project altogether unfit for a nation of shopkeepers; but extremely fit for a nation whose government is influenced by shopkeepers. Such statesmen, and such statesmen only, are capable of fancying that they will find some advantage in employing the blood and treasure of their fellow-citizens to found and maintain such an empire.

WN 579, 580

The monopoly of the colony trade besides, by forcing towards it a much greater proportion of the capital of Great Britain than what would naturally have gone to it, seems to have broken altogether that natural balance which would otherwise have taken place among all the different branches of British industry. The industry of Great Britain, instead of being accommodated to a great number of small markets, has been principally suited to one great market. Her commerce, instead of running in a great number of small channels, has been taught to run principally in one great channel. But the whole system of her industry and commerce has thereby been rendered less secure, the whole state of her body politic less healthful than it otherwise would have been. In her present condition, Great Britain resembles one of those unwholesome bodies in which some of the vital parts are overgrown, and which, upon that account, are liable to many dangerous disorders scarce incident to those in which all the parts are more properly proportioned. A small stop in that great blood-vessel, which has been artificially swelled beyond its natural dimensions, and through which an unnatural proportion of the industry and commerce of the country has been forced to circulate, is very likely to bring on the most dangerous disorders upon the whole body politic. . . .

Some moderate and gradual relaxation of the laws which give to Great Britain the exclusive trade to the colonies, till it is rendered in a great measure free, seems to be the only expedient which can, in all future times, deliver her from this danger, which can enable her or even force her to withdraw some part of her capital from this overgrown employment, and to turn it, though with less profit, towards other employments; and which, by gradually diminishing one branch of her industry and gradually increasing all the rest, can by degrees restore all the different branches of it to that natural, healthful, and proper proportion which perfect liberty necessarily establishes, and which perfect liberty can alone preserve.

WN 570–572

Though the policy of Great Britain with regard to the trade of her colonies has been dictated by the same mercantile spirit as that of other nations, it has, however, upon the whole, been less illiberal and oppressive than that of any of them.

In everything, except their foreign trade, the liberty of the English colonists to manage their own affairs their own way is complete. It is in every respect equal to that of their fellow-citizens at home, and is secured in the same manner, by an assembly of the representatives of the people, who claim the sole right of imposing taxes for the support of the colony government.

WN 551

To propose that Great Britain should voluntarily give up all authority over her colonies, and leave them to elect their own magistrates, to enact their own laws, and to make peace and war as they might think proper, would be to propose such a measure as never was, and never will be adopted, by any nation in the world. No nation ever voluntarily gave up the dominion of any province, how troublesome soever it might be to govern it, and how small soever the revenue which it afforded might be in proportion to the expense which it occasioned. Such sacrifices, though they might frequently be agreeable to the interest, are always mortifying to the pride of every nation, and what is perhaps of still greater consequence, they are always contrary to the private interest of the governing part of it, who would thereby be deprived of the disposal of many places of trust and profit, of many opportunities of acquiring wealth and distinction, which the possession of the most turbulent, and, to the great body of the people, the most unprofitable province seldom fails to afford. The most visionary enthusiast would scarce be capable of proposing such a measure with any serious hopes at least of its ever being adopted. If it was adopted, however, Great Britain would not only be immediately freed from the whole annual expense of the peace establishment of the colonies, but might settle with them such a treaty of commerce as would effectually secure to her a free trade, more advantageous to the great body of the people, though less so to the merchants, than the monopoly which she at present enjoys. By thus parting good friends, the natural affection of the colonies to the mother country which, perhaps, our late dissensions have well nigh extinguished, would quickly revive. It might dispose them not only to respect, for whole centuries together, that treaty of commerce which they had concluded with us at parting, but to favour us in war as well as in trade, and, instead of turbulent and factious subjects, to become our most faithful, affectionate, and generous allies; and the same sort of parental affection on the one side, and filial respect on the other, might revive between Great Britain and her colonies, which used to subsist between those of ancient Greece and the mother city from which they descended.

WN 581, 582

Plenty of good land, and liberty to manage their own affairs their own way, seem to be the two great causes of the prosperity of all new colonies.

WN 538

The policy of Europe . . . has very little to boast of, either in the original establishment or, so far as concerns their internal government, in the subsequent prosperity of the colonies of America.

Folly and injustice seem to have been the principles which presided over and directed the first project of establishing those colonies; the folly of hunting after gold and silver mines, and the injustice of coveting the possession of a country whose harmless natives, far from having ever injured the people of Europe, had received the first adventurers with every mark of kindness and hospitality.

The adventurers, indeed, who formed some of the later establishments, joined to the chimerical project of finding gold and silver mines other motives more reasonable and more laudable; but even these motives do very little honour to the policy of Europe.

The English puritans, restrained at home, fled for free-

dom to America, and established there the four governments of New England. The English Catholics, treated
with much greater injustice, established that of Maryland;
the Quakers, that of Pennsylvania. The Portuguese Jews,
persecuted by the inquisition, stripped of their fortunes,
and banished to Brazil, introduced by their example some
sort of order and industry among the transported felons
and strumpets by whom that colony was originally
peopled, and taught them the culture of the sugar-cane.
Upon all these different occasions it was not the wisdom
and policy, but the disorder and injustice of the European
governments which peopled and cultivated America.

WN 555

In what way . . . has the policy of Europe contributed
either to the first establishment, or to the present grandeur
of the colonies of America? In one way, and in one way
only, it has contributed a good deal. Magna virum Mater!
It bred and formed the men who were capable of achiev-
ing such great actions, and of laying the foundation of so
great an empire; and there is no other quarter of the world
of which the policy is capable of forming, or has ever
actually and in fact formed such men. The colonies owe
to the policy of Europe the education and great views of
their active and enterprising founders; and some of the
greatest and most important of them, so far as concerns
their internal government, owe to it scarce anything else.

WN 556

Men desire to have some share in the management of public affairs chiefly on account of the importance which it gives them. Upon the power which the greater part of the leading men, the natural aristocracy of every country, have of preserving or defending their respective importance, depends the stability and duration of every system of free government. In the attacks which those leading men are continually making upon the importance of one another, and in the defence of their own, consists the whole play of domestic faction and ambition. The leading men of America, like those of all other countries, desire to preserve their own importance. They feel, or imagine, that if their assemblies, which they are fond of calling parliaments, and of considering as equal in authority to the parliament of Great Britain, should be so far degraded as to become the humble ministers and executive officers of that parliament, the greater part of their own importance would be at end. They have rejected, therefore, the proposal of being taxed by parliamentary requisition, and like other ambitious and high-spirited men, have rather chosen to draw the sword in defence of their own importance.

WN 586, 587

The parliament of Great Britain insists upon taxing the colonies; and they refuse to be taxed by a parliament in which they are not represented. If to each colony, which should detach itself from the general confederacy, Great Britain should allow such a number of representatives as suited the proportion of what is contributed to the public revenue of the empire, in consequence of its being subjected to the same taxes, and in compensation admitted to the same freedom of trade with its fellow-subjects at home; the number of its representatives to be augmented as the proportion of its contribution might afterwards augment; a new method of acquiring importance, a new and more dazzling object of ambition would be presented to the leading men of each colony. Instead of piddling for the little prizes which are to be found in what may be called the paltry raffle of colony faction; they might then hope, from the presumption which men naturally have in their own ability and good fortune, to draw some of the great prizes which sometimes come from the wheel of the great state lottery of British politics. Unless this or some other method is fallen upon, and there seems to be none more obvious than this, of preserving the importance and gratifying the ambition of the leading men of America, it is not very probable that they will ever voluntarily submit to us; and we ought to consider that the blood which must be shed in forcing them to do so is, every drop of it, the blood either of those who are, or of those whom we wish to have for our fellow-citizens. They are very weak who flatter themselves that, in the state to which things have come, our colonies will be easily conquered by force alone. The persons who now govern the resolutions of what they call their continental congress, feel in themselves at this moment a degree of importance which, perhaps, the greatest subjects in Europe scarce feel. From shopkeepers, tradesmen, and attornies, they are become statesmen and legislators, and are employed in contriving a new form of government for an extensive empire, which, they flatter themselves, will become and which, indeed, seems very likely to become, one of the greatest and most formidable that ever was in the world. Five hundred different people, perhaps, who in different ways act immediately under the continental congress; and five hundred thousand, perhaps, who act under those five hundred, all feel in the same manner a proportionable rise in their own importance. Almost every individual of the governing party in America fills, at present in his own fancy, a station superior, not only to what he had ever filled before, but to what he had ever expected to fill; and unless some new object of ambition is presented either to him or to his leaders, if he has the ordinary spirit of a man, he will die in defence of that station.

WN 587, 588

No oppressive aristocracy has ever prevailed in the colonies. Even they, however, would in point of happiness and tranquillity, gain considerably by a union with Great Britain. It would, at least, deliver them from those rancorous and virulent factions which are inseparable from small democracies, and which have so frequently divided the affections of their people, and disturbed the tranquillity of their governments, in their form so nearly democratical.

WN 897

The rulers of Great Britain have, for more than a century past, amused the people with the imagination that they possessed a great empire on the west side of the Atlantic. This empire, however, has hitherto existed in imagination only. It has hitherto been, not an empire, but the project of an empire; not a gold mine, but the project of a gold mine; a project which has cost, which continues to cost, and which, if pursued in the same way as it has been hitherto, is likely to cost, immense expense, without being likely to bring any profit; for the effects of the monopoly of the colony trade, it has been shown, are, to the great body of the people, mere loss instead of profit. It is surely now time that our rulers should either realise this golden dream, in which they have been indulging themselves, perhaps, as well as the people, or that they should awake from it themselves, and endeavour to awaken the people. If the project cannot be completed, it ought to be given up. If any of the provinces of the British empire cannot be made to contribute towards the support of the whole empire, it is surely time that Great Britain should free herself from the expense of defending those provinces in time of war, and of supporting any part of their civil or military establishments in time of peace, and endeavour to accommodate her future views and designs to the real mediocrity of her circumstances.

WN 899, 900

19

War

An industrious, and upon that account a wealthy nation, is of all nations the most likely to be attacked; and unless the state takes some new measures for the public defence, the natural habits of the people render them altogether incapable of defending themselves.

WN 659

The fall of the Greek republics and of the Persian empire, was the effect of the irresistible superiority which a standing army has over every sort of militia. It is the first great revolution in the affairs of mankind, of which history has preserved any distinct or circumstantial account.

The fall of Carthage, and the consequent elevation of Rome, is the second. All the varieties of the fortune of those two famous republics may very well be accounted for from the same cause.

WN 663

War and the preparation for war, are the two circumstances which in modern times occasion the greater part of the necessary expence of all great states.

WN 773

When the art of war, too, has gradually grown up to be a very intricate and complicated science, when the event of war ceases to be determined, as in the first ages of society, by a single irregular skirmish or battle, but when the contest is generally spun out through several different campaigns, each of which lasts during the greater part of the year, it becomes universally necessary that the public should maintain those who serve the public in war, at least while they are employed in that service. Whatever in time of peace might be the ordinary occupation of those who go to war, so very tedious and expensive a service would otherwise be by far too heavy a burden upon them.

WN 657

Among the civilized nations of modern Europe, it is commonly computed, that not more than one hundredth part of the inhabitants of any country can be employed as soldiers, without ruin to the country which pays the expence of their service.

WN 657, 658

The security of every society must always depend, more or less, upon the martial spirit of the great body of the people. In the present times, indeed, that martial spirit alone, and unsupported by a well-disciplined standing army, would not, perhaps be sufficient for the defence and security of any society. But where every citizen had the spirit of a soldier, a small standing army would surely be requisite. That spirit, besides, would necessarily diminish very much the dangers to liberty, whether real or imaginary, which are commonly apprehended from a standing army. As it would very much facilitate the operations of that army against a foreign invader, so it would obstruct them as much if unfortunately they should ever be directed against the constitution of the state.

WN 738, 739

In modern war the great expense of firearms gives an evident advantage to the nation which can best afford that expense, and consequently to an opulent and civilised over a poor and barbarous nation. In ancient times the opulent and civilised found it difficult to defend themselves against the poor and barbarous nations. In modern times the poor and barbarous find it difficult to defend themselves against the opulent and civilised. The invention of firearms, an invention which at first sight appears to be so pernicious, is certainly favourable both to the permanency and to the extension of civilisation.

WN 669

A well-regulated standing army is superior to every militia. Such an army, as it can best be maintained by an opulent and civilised nation, so it can alone defend such a nation against the invasion of a poor and barbarous neighbour. It is only by means of a standing army, therefore, that the civilisation of any country can be perpetuated, or even preserved for any considerable time.

WN 667

The soldiers, who are bound to obey their officer only once a week or once a month, and who are at all other times at liberty to manage their own affairs their own way, without being in any respect accountable to him, can never be under the same awe in his presence, can never have the same disposition to ready obedience, with those whose whole life and conduct are every day directed by him, and who every day even rise and go to bed, or at least retire to their quarters, according to his orders. In what is called discipline, or in the habit of ready obedience, a militia must always be still more inferior to a standing army, than it may sometimes be in what is called the manual exercise, or in the management and use of its arms. But in modern war the habit of ready and instant obedience is of much greater consequence than a considerable superiority in the management of arms.

WN 662

Regularity, order, and prompt obedience to command are qualities which, in modern armies, are of more importance towards determining the fate of battles than the dexterity and skill of the soldiers in the use of their arms.

But the noise of firearms, the smoke, and the invisible death to which every man feels himself every moment exposed as soon as he comes within cannon-shot, and frequently a long time before the battle can be well said to be engaged, must render it very difficult to maintain any considerable degree of this regularity, order, and prompt obedience, even in the beginning of a modern battle. In an ancient battle there was no noise but what arose from the human voice; there was no smoke, there was no invisible cause of wounds or death. Every man, till some mortal weapon actually did approach him, saw clearly that no such weapon was near him. In these circumstances, and among troops who had some confidence in their own skill and dexterity in the use of their arms, it must have been a good deal less difficult to preserve some degree of regularity and order, not only in the beginning, but through the whole progress of an ancient battle, and till one of the two armies was fairly defeated. But the habits of regularity, order, and prompt obedience to command can be acquired only by troops which are exercised in great bodies.

WN 661

When a young officer exposes his life to acquire some inconsiderable addition to the dominions of his sovereign, it is not because the acquisition of the new territory is to himself an object more desirable than the preservation of his own life. To him his own life is of infinitely more value than the conquest of a whole kingdom for the state which he serves. But when he compares those two objects with one another, he does not view them in the light in which they naturally appear to himself, but in that in which they appear to the nation he fights for. To them the success of the war is of the highest importance — the life of a private person of scarce any consequence. When he puts himself in their situation, he immediately feels that he cannot be too prodigal of his blood, if by shedding it he can promote so valuable a purpose. In thus thwarting, from a sense of duty and propriety, the strongest of all natural propensities, consists the heroism of his conduct. There is many an honest Englishman, who in his private station would be more seriously disturbed by the loss of a guinea than by the national loss of Minorca, who yet, had it been in his power to defend that fortress, would have sacrificed his life a thousand times rather than, through his fault, have let it fall into the hands of the enemy.

MS 314, 315

Death, as we say, is the king of terrors; and the man who has conquered the fear of death is not likely to lose his presence of mind at the approach of any other natural evil.

MS 389

Nothing can be more contemptible than an Indian war in North America.

WN 655

20

Patriotism

We do not love our country merely as a part of the great society of mankind — we love it for its own sake, and independently of any such consideration. That wisdom which contrived the system of human affections, as well as that of every other part of nature, seems to have judged that the interest of the great society of mankind would be best promoted by directing the principal attention of each individual to that particular portion of it which was most within the sphere both of his abilities and of his understanding.

MS 375

The patriot who lays down his life for the safety, or even for the vainglory of this society, appears to act with the most exact propriety. He appears to view himself in the light in which the impartial spectator naturally and necessarily views him, as but one of the multitude, in the eye of that equitable judge, of no more consequence than any other in it, but bound at all times to sacrifice and devote himself to the safety, to the service, and even to the glory, of the greater number. But though this sacrifice appears to be perfectly just and proper, we know how difficult it is to make it, and how few people are capable of making it. His conduct, therefore, excites not only our entire approbation but our highest wonder and admiration, and seems to merit all the applause which can be due to the most heroic virtue. The traitor, on the contrary, who, in some peculiar situation, fancies he can promote his own little interest by betraying to the public enemy that of his native country; who, regardless of the judgment of the man within the breast, prefers himself, in this respect, so shamefully and so basely, to all those with whom he has any connection, appears to be of all villains the most detestable.

MS 373

The love of our own country seems not to be derived from the love of mankind. The former sentiment is altogether independent of the latter, and seems sometimes even to dispose us to act inconsistently with it. France may contain, perhaps, near three times the number of inhabitants which Great Britain contains. In the great society of mankind, therefore, the prosperity of France should appear to be an object of much greater importance than that of Great Britain. The British subject, however, who upon that account should prefer upon all occasions the prosperity of the former to that of the latter country, would not be thought a good citizen of Great Britain.

MS 375

The regard for the laws of nations, or for those rules which independent states profess or pretend to think themselves bound to observe in their dealings with one another, is often very little more than mere pretence and profession. From the smallest interest, upon the slightest provocation, we see those rules every day either evaded or directly violated without shame or remorse. Each nation foresees, or imagines it foresees, its own subjugation in the increasing power and aggrandisement of any of its neighbours; and the mean principle of national prejudice is often founded upon the noble one of the love of our own country.

MS 373, 374

Of the conduct of one independent nation towards another, neutral nations are the only indifferent and impartial spectators. But they are placed at so great a distance that they are almost quite out of sight. When two nations are at variance, the citizen of each pays little regard to the sentiments which foreign nations may entertain concerning his conduct. His whole ambition is to obtain the approbation of his fellow-citizens; and, as they are all animated by the same hostile passions which animate himself, he can never please them so much as by enraging and offending their enemies. The partial spectator is at hand: the impartial one at a great distance. In war and negotiation, therefore, the laws of justice are very seldom observed. Truth and fair dealing are almost totally disregarded. Treaties are violated; and the violation, if some advantage is gained by it, sheds scarce any dishonour upon the violator. The ambassador who dupes the minister of a foreign nation is admired and applauded. The just man who disdains either to take or to give any disadvantage, but who would think it less dishonourable to give than to take one — the man who in all private transactions would be the most beloved and the most esteemed, in those public transactions is regarded as a fool and an idiot, who does not understand his business, and he incurs always the contempt, and sometimes even the detestation, of his fellow citizens. In war, not only what are called the laws of nations are frequently violated, without bringing (among his own fellow-citizens, whose judgments he only regards) any considerable dishonour upon the violator; but those laws themselves are, the greater part of them, laid down with very little regard to the plainest and most obvious rules of justice. That the innocent, though they may have some connection or dependency upon the guilty (which, perhaps, they themselves cannot help), should not upon that account suffer or be punished for the guilty, is one of the plainest and most obvious rules of justice. In the most unjust war, however, it is commonly the sovereign or the rulers only who are guilty. The subjects are almost always perfectly

innocent. Whenever it suits the convenience of a public
enemy, however, the goods of the peaceable citizens are
seized both at land and at sea; their lands are laid waste,
their houses are burnt, and they themselves, if they presume to make any resistance, are murdered or led into
captivity; and all this in the most perfect conformity to
what are called the laws of nations.

MS 258, 259

The love of our country seems, in ordinary cases, to
involve in it two different principles; first, a certain respect and reverence for that constitution or form of government which is actually established; and, secondly, an
earnest desire to render the condition of our fellow-
citizens as safe, respectable, and happy as we can. He is
not a citizen who is not disposed to respect the laws and
to obey the civil magistrate; and he is certainly not a good
citizen who does not wish to promote, by every means in
his power, the welfare of the whole society of his fellow-
citizens.

In peaceable and quiet times those two principles generally coincide and lead to the same conduct. The support
of the established government seems evidently the best
expedient for maintaining the safe, respectable, and
happy situation of our fellow-citizens — when we see
that this government actually maintains them in that situation. But in times of public discontent, faction, and disorder, those two different principles may draw different
ways, and even a wise man may be disposed to think

some alteration necessary in that constitution or form of government which, in its actual condition, appears plainly unable to maintain the public tranquility. In such cases, however, it often requires, perhaps, the highest effort of political wisdom to determine when a real patriot ought to support and endeavour to re-establish the authority of the old system, and when he ought to give way to the more daring, but often dangerous, spirit of innovation.

MS 377, 378

Though our effectual good offices can very seldom be extended to any wider society than that of our own country, our good will is circumscribed by no boundary, but may embrace the immensity of the universe.

MS 383

21

Ambition

Those great objects of self-interest, of which the loss or acquisition quite changes the rank of the person, are the objects of the passion properly called ambition; a passion which, when it keeps within the bounds of prudence and justice, is always admired in the world, and has even sometimes a certain irregular greatness, which dazzles the imagination when it passes the limits of both these virtues, and is not only unjust but extravagant. Hence the general admiration for heroes and conquerors, and even for statesmen, whose projects have been very daring and extensive, though altogether devoid of justice; such as those of the cardinals of Richelieu and of Retz. The objects of avarice and ambition differ only in their greatness. A miser is as furious about a halfpenny as a man of ambition about the conquest of a kingdom.

MS 287

The desire of being believed, the desire of persuading, of leading, and directing other people, seems to be one of the strongest of all our natural desires. It is perhaps the instinct upon which is founded the faculty of speech, the characteristical faculty of human nature. No other animal possesses this faculty, and we cannot discover in any other animal any desire to lead and direct the judgment and conduct of its fellows. Great ambition, the desire of real superiority, of leading and directing, seems to be altogether peculiar to man, and speech is the great instrument of ambition, of real superiority, of leading and directing the judgments and conduct of other people.

MS 529, 530

"Love," says my Lord Rochefoucault, "is commonly succeeded by ambition, but ambition is hardly ever succeeded by love." That passion, when once it has got entire possession of the breast, will admit neither a rival nor a successor. To those who have been accustomed to the possession, or even to the hope, of public admiration, all other pleasures sicken and decay. Of all the discarded statesmen who, for their own ease, have studied to get the better of ambition, and to despise those honours which they could no longer arrive at, how few have been able to succeed? The greater part have spent their time in the most listless and insipid indolence, chagrined at the thoughts of their own insignificancy, incapable of being interested in the occupations of private life, without enjoyment, except when they talked of their former greatness, and without satisfaction, except when they were employed in some vain project to recover it. Are you in earnest resolved never to barter your liberty for the lordly servitude of a court, but to live free, fearless, and independent? There seems to be one way to continue in that virtuous resolution; and perhaps but one. Never enter the place from whence so few have been able to return; never come within the circle of ambition; nor ever bring yourself into comparison with those masters of the earth who have already engrossed the attention of half mankind before you.

MS 122

It is because mankind are disposed to sympathize more entirely with our joy than with our sorrow, that we make parade of our riches, and conceal our poverty. Nothing is so mortifying as to be obliged to expose our distress to the view of the public, and to feel, that though our situation is open to the eyes of all mankind, no mortal conceives for us the half of what we suffer. Nay, it is chiefly from this regard to the sentiments of mankind, that we pursue riches and avoid poverty. For to what purpose is all the toil and bustle of this world? what is the end of avarice and ambition, of the pursuit of wealth, of power, and pre-eminence? Is it to supply the necessities of nature? the wages of the meanest labourer can supply them. We see that they afford him food and clothing, the comfort of a house, and of a family. If we examine his economy with rigour, we should find that he spends a great part of them upon conveniences, which may be regarded as super-fluities, and that, upon extraordinary occasions, he can give something even to vanity and distinction. What then is the cause of our aversion to his situation, and why should those who have been educated in the higher ranks of life, regard it as worse than death, to be reduced to live, even without labour, upon the same simple fare with him, to dwell under the same lowly roof, and to be clothed in the same humble attire? Do they imagine that their stomach is better, or their sleep sounder, in a palace than in a cottage? The contrary has been so often observed, and, indeed, is so very obvious, though it had never been observed, that there is nobody ignorant of it. For whence, then, arises that emulation which runs through all the different ranks of men, and what are the advantages which we propose by that great purpose of human life which we call bettering our condition? To be observed, to be attended to, to be taken notice of with sympathy, complacency, and approbation, are all the advantages which we can propose to derive from it. It is the vanity, not the ease, or the pleasure, which interests us.

MS 112, 113

Place, that great object which divides the wives of aldermen, is the end of half the labours of human life; and is the cause of all the tumult and bustle, all the rapine and injustice, which avarice and ambition have introduced into this world.

MS 122, 123

In many governments the candidates for the highest stations are above the law; and, if they can attain the object of their ambition, they have no fear of being called to account for the means by which they acquire it. They often endeavour, therefore, not only by fraud and falsehood, the ordinary and vulgar arts of intrigue and cabal, but sometimes by the perpetration of the most enormous crimes, by murder and assassination, by rebellion and civil war, to supplant and destroy those who oppose or stand in the way of their greatness. They more frequently miscarry than succeed; and commonly gain nothing but the disgraceful punishment which is due to their crimes. But, though they should be so lucky as to attain that wished-for greatness, they are always most miserably disappointed in the happiness which they expect to enjoy in it.

MS 130, 131

The poor man's son, whom heaven in its anger has visited with ambition, when he begins to look around him, admires the condition of the rich. He finds the cottage of his father too small for his accommodation, and fancies he should be lodged more at his ease in a palace. He is displeased with being obliged to walk afoot, or to endure the fatigue of riding on horseback. He sees his superiors carried about in machines, and imagines that in one of these he could travel with less inconveniency. He feels himself naturally indolent, and willing to serve himself with his own hands as little as possible; and judges that a numerous retinue of servants would save him from a great deal of trouble. He thinks if he has attained all these, he would sit still contentedly, and be quiet, enjoying himself in the thought of the happiness and tranquillity of his situation. He is enchanted with the distant idea of this felicity. It appears in his fancy like the life of some superior rank of beings, and, in order to arrive at it, he devotes himself for ever to the pursuit of wealth and greatness. To obtain the conveniencies which these afford, he submits in the first year, nay, in the first month of his application, to more fatigue of body and more uneasiness of mind, than he could have suffered through the whole of his life from the want of them. He studies to distinguish himself in some laborious profession. With the most unrelenting industry he labours night and day to acquire talents superior to all his competitors. He endeavours next to bring those talents into public view, and with equal assiduity solicits every opportunity of employment. For this purpose he makes his court to all mankind; he serves those whom he hates, and is obsequious to those whom he despises. Through the whole of his life he pursues the idea of a certain artificial and elegant repose which he may never arrive at, for which he sacrifices a real tranquillity that is at all times in his power, and which, if in the extremity of old age he should at last attain to it, he will find to be in no respect preferable to that humble security and contentment which he had abandoned for it. It is then, in the last dregs of life, his body wasted with toil and diseases, his mind galled and ruffled by the memory of a thousand injuries and disappointments which he imagines he had met with from the injustice of his enemies, or from the perfidy and ingratitude of his friends, that he begins at last to find that wealth and greatness are mere trinkets of frivolous utility, no more adapted for procuring ease of body or tranquillity of mind, than the tweezer-cases of the lover of toys.

MS 299–301

In the most glittering and exalted situation that our idle fancy can hold out to us, the pleasures from which we propose to derive our real happiness are almost always the same with those which, in our actual though humble station, we have at all times at hand and in our power. Except the frivolous pleasures of vanity and superiority, we may find, in the most humble station, where there is only personal liberty, every other which the most exalted can afford; and the pleasures of vanity and superiority are seldom consistent with perfect tranquillity, the principle and foundation of all real and satisfactory enjoyment.

MS 251, 252

22

Government

What institution of government could tend so much to promote the happiness of mankind as the general prevalence of wisdom and virtue? All government is but an imperfect remedy for the deficiency of these.

MS 308

Among nations of hunters, as there is scarce any property, or at least none that exceeds the value of two or three days' labour, so there is seldom any established magistrate or any regular administration of justice. Men who have no property can injure one another only in their persons or reputations. But when one man kills, wounds, beats, or defames another, though he to whom the injury is done suffers, he who does it receives no benefit. It is otherwise with the injuries to property. The benefit of the person who does the injury is often equal to the loss of him who suffers it. Envy, malice, or resentment are the only passions which can prompt one man to injure another in his person or reputation. But the greater part of men are not very frequently under the influence of those passions, and at the very worst men are so only occasionally. As their gratification too, how agreeable soever it may be to certain characters, is not attended with any real or permanent advantage, it is in the greater part of men commonly restrained by prudential considerations. Men may live together in society with some tolerable degree of security, though there is no civil magistrate to protect them from the injustice of those passions. But avarice and ambition in the rich, in the poor the hatred of labour and the love of present ease and enjoyment, are the passions which prompt to invade property, passions much more steady in their operation, and much more universal in their influence. Wherever there is great property there is great inequality. For one very rich man there must be at least five hundred poor, and the affluence of the few supposes the indigence of the many. The affluence of the rich excites the indignation of the poor, who are often both driven by want, and prompted by envy, to invade his possessions. It is only under the shelter of the civil magistrate that the owner of that valuable property, which is acquired by the labour of many years, or perhaps of many successive generations, can sleep a single night in security. He is at all times surrounded by unknown enemies, whom, though he never provoked, he can never appease, and from whose injustice he can be protected only by the powerful arm of the civil magistrate continually held up to chastise it. The acquisition of valuable and extensive property, therefore, necessarily requires the establishment of civil government.

WN 669, 670

Civil government, so far as it is instituted for the security of property, is in reality instituted for the defence of the rich against the poor, or of those who have some property against those who have none at all.

WN 674

The authority of riches, however, though great in every age of society, is perhaps greatest in the rudest age of society which admits of any considerable inequality of fortune. A Tartar chief, the increase of whose herds and stocks is sufficient to maintain a thousand men, cannot well employ that increase in any other way than in maintaining a thousand men. The rude state of his society does not afford him any manufactured produce, any trinkets or baubles of any kind, for which he can exchange that part of his rude produce which is over and above his own consumption. The thousand men whom he thus maintains, depending entirely upon him for their subsistence, must both obey his orders in war, and submit to his jurisdiction in peace. He is necessarily both their general and their judge, and his chieftainship is the necessary effect of the superiority of his fortune. In an opulent and civilised society, a man may possess a much greater fortune and yet not be able to command a dozen of people. Though the produce of his estate may be sufficient to maintain, and may perhaps actually maintain, more than a thousand people, yet as those people pay for everything which they get from him, as he gives scarce anything to anybody but in exchange for an equivalent, there is scarce anybody who considers himself as entirely dependent upon him, and his authority extends only over a few menial servants. . . .

All families are equally ancient; and the ancestors of the prince, though they may be better known, cannot well be more numerous than those of the beggar. Antiquity of family means everywhere the antiquity either of wealth, or of that greatness which is commonly either founded upon wealth, or accompanied with it. Upstart greatness is everywhere less respected than ancient greatness. The hatred of usurpers, the love of the family of an ancient monarch, are, in a great measure, founded upon the contempt which men naturally have for the former, and upon their veneration for the latter.

WN 671, 672

The proud minister of an ostentatious court may frequently take pleasure in executing a work of splendour and magnificence, such as a great highway, which is frequently seen by the principal nobility, whose applauses not only flatter his vanity, but even contribute to support his interest at court. But to execute a great number of little works, in which nothing that can be done can make any great appearance, or excite the smallest degree of admiration in any traveller, and which, in short, have nothing to recommend them but their extreme utility, is a business which appears in every respect too mean and paltry to merit the attention of so great a magistrate. Under such an administration, therefore, such works are almost always entirely neglected.

WN 687

Every system which endeavours, either by extraordinary encouragements to draw towards a particular species of industry a greater share of the capital of the society than what would naturally go to it, or, by extraordinary restraints, force from a particular species of industry some share of the capital which would otherwise be employed in it, is in reality subversive of the great purpose which it means to promote. It retards, instead of accelerating, the progress of the society towards real wealth and greatness; and diminishes, instead of increasing, the real value of the annual produce of its land and labour.

All systems either of preference or of restraint, therefore, being thus completely taken away, the obvious and simple system of natural liberty establishes itself of its own accord. Every man, as long as he does not violate the laws of justice, is left perfectly free to pursue his own interest his own way, and to bring both his industry and capital into competition with those of any other man, or order of men. The sovereign is completely discharged from a duty, in the attempting to perform which he must always be exposed to innumerable delusions, and for the proper performance of which no human wisdom or knowledge could ever be sufficient; the duty of superintending the industry of private people, and of directing it towards the employments most suitable to the interest of the society. According to the system of natural liberty, the sovereign has only three duties to attend to; three duties of great importance, indeed, but plain and intelligible to common understandings: first, the duty of protecting the society from the violence and invasion of other independent societies; secondly, the duty of protecting, as far as possible, every member of the society from the injustice or oppression of every other member of it, or the duty of establishing an exact administration of justice; and, thirdly, the duty of erecting and maintaining certain public works and certain public institutions which it can never be for the interest of any individual, or small number of individuals, to erect and maintain; because the profit could never repay the expense to any individual or small number of individuals, though it may frequently do much more than repay it to a great society.

WN 650, 651

The third and last duty of the sovereign or commonwealth is that of erecting and maintaining those public institutions and those public works, which, though they may be in the highest degree advantageous to a great society, are, however, of such a nature, that the profit could never repay the expense to any individual or small number of individuals, and which it therefore cannot be expected that any individual or small number of individuals should erect or maintain.

WN 681

Even those public works which are of such a nature that they cannot afford any revenue for maintaining themselves, but of which the conveniency is nearly confined to some particular place or district, are always better maintained by a local or provincial revenue, under the management of a local and provincial administration, than by the general revenue of the state, of which the executive power must always have the management. Were the streets of London to be lighted and paved at the expense of the treasury, is there any probability that they would be so well lighted and paved as they are at present, or even at so small an expense? The expense, besides, instead of being raised by a local tax upon the inhabitants of each particular street, parish, or district in London, would, in this case, be defrayed out of the general revenue of the state, and would consequently be raised by a tax upon all the inhabitants of the kingdom, of whom the greater part derive no sort of benefit from the lighting and paving of the streets of London.

WN 689

The abuses which sometimes creep into the local and provincial administration of a local and provincial revenue, how enormous soever they may appear, are in reality, however, almost always very trifling in comparison of those which commonly take place in the administration and expenditure of the revenue of a great empire. They are, besides, much more easily corrected.

WN 689

When high roads, bridges, canals, &c. are in this manner made and supported by the commerce which is carried on by means of them, they can be made only where that commerce requires them, and consequently where it is proper to make them. Their expense too, their grandeur and magnificence, must be suited to what that commerce can afford to pay. They must be made consequently as it is proper to make them. A magnificent high road cannot be made through a desert country where there is little or no commerce, or merely because it happens to lead to the country villa of the intendant of the province, or to that of some great lord to whom the intendant finds it convenient to make his court. A great bridge cannot be thrown over a river at a place where nobody passes, or merely to embellish the view from the windows of a neighbouring palace: things which sometimes happen, in countries where works of this kind are carried on by any other revenue than that which they themselves are capable of affording.

WN 683

The post office is properly a mercantile project. The government advances the expense of establishing the different offices, and of buying or hiring the necessary horses or carriages, and is repaid with a large profit by the duties upon what is carried. It is perhaps the only mercantile project which has been successfully managed by, I believe, every sort of government. The capital to be advanced is not very considerable. There is no mystery in the business. The returns are not only certain, but immediate.

WN 770, 771

In all governments accordingly, even in monarchies, the highest offices are generally possessed, and the whole detail of the administration conducted, by men who were educated in the middle and inferior ranks of life, who have been carried forward by their own industry and abilities, though loaded with the jealousy, and opposed by the resentment, of all those who were born their superiors, and to whom the great, after having regarded them, first with contempt and afterwards with envy, are at last contented to truckle with the same abject meanness with which they desire that the rest of mankind should behave to themselves.

MS 120, 121

Public services are never better performed than when their reward comes only in consequence of their being performed, and is proportioned to the diligence employed in performing them.

WN 678

The emoluments of officers are not, like those of trades and professions, regulated by the free competition of the market, and do not, therefore, always bear a just proportion to what the nature of the employment requires. They are, perhaps, in most countries, higher than it requires; the persons who have the administration of government being generally disposed to reward both themselves and their immediate dependents rather more than enough.

WN 818

There is no art which one government sooner learns of another, than that of draining money from the pockets of the people.

WN 813

When national debts have once been accumulated to a certain degree, there is scarce, I believe, a single instance of their having been fairly and completely paid. The liberation of the public revenue, if it has ever been brought about at all, has always been brought about by a bankruptcy; sometimes by an avowed one, but always by a real one, though frequently by a pretended payment.

The raising of the denomination of the coin has been the most usual expedient by which a real public bankruptcy has been disguised under the appearance of a pretended payment.

WN 882

A pretended payment of this kind, therefore, instead of alleviating, aggravates in most cases the loss of the creditors of the public; and without any advantage to the public, extends the calamity to a great number of other innocent people. It occasions a general and most pernicious subversion of the fortunes of private people; enriching in most cases the idle and profuse debtor at the expense of the industrious and frugal creditor, and transporting a great part of the national capital from the hands which were likely to increase and improve it, to those which are likely to dissipate and destroy it. When it becomes necessary for a state to declare itself bankrupt, in the same manner as when it becomes necessary for an individual to do so, a fair, open, and avowed bankruptcy is always the measure which is both least dishonourable to the debtor, and least hurtful to the creditor. The honour of a state is surely very poorly provided for, when, in order to cover the disgrace of a real bankruptcy, it has recourse to a juggling trick of this kind, so easily seen through, and at the same time so extremely pernicious.

WN 883

Whoever examines, with attention, the history of the dearths and famines which have afflicted any part of Europe, during either the course of the present or that of the two preceding centuries, of several of which we have pretty exact accounts, will find, I believe, that a dearth never has arisen from any combination among the inland dealers in corn, nor from any other cause but a real scar-

city, occasioned sometimes, perhaps, and in some particular places, by the waste of war, but in far the greatest
number of cases, by the fault of the seasons; and that a
famine has never arisen from any other cause but the
violence of government attempting, by improper means,
to remedy the inconveniencies of a dearth.

WN 492, 493

When the government, in order to remedy the inconveniencies of dearth, orders all the dealers to sell their
corn at what it supposes a reasonable price, it either
hinders them from bringing it to market, which may
sometimes produce a famine even in the beginning of the
season; or if they bring it thither, it enables the people,
and thereby encourages them to consume it so fast, as
must necessarily produce a famine before the end of the
season. The unlimited, unrestrained freedom of the corn
trade, as it is the only effectual preventative of the miseries of a famine, so it is the best palliative of the inconveniencies of a dearth; for the inconveniencies of a real
scarcity cannot be remedied; they can only be palliated.
No trade deserves more the full protection of the law, and
no trade requires it so much; because no trade is so much
exposed to popular odium.

WN 493

To relieve the present exigency is always the object
which principally interests those immediately concerned
in the administration of public affairs. The future libera-

tion of the public revenue, they leave to the care of posterity.

WN 867, 868

In the progress of despotism the authority of the executive power gradually absorbs that of every other power in the state, and assumes to itself the management of every branch of revenue which is destined for any public purpose.

WN 687

Fear is in almost all cases a wretched instrument of government, and ought in particular never to be employed against any order of men who have the smallest pretensions to independency. To attempt to terrify them serves only to irritate their bad humour, and to confirm them in an opposition which more gentle usage perhaps might easily induce them either to soften, or to lay aside altogether.

WN 750, 751

What is the species of domestic industry which his capital can employ, and of which the produce is likely to be of the greatest value, every individual, it is evident, can, in his local situation, judge much better than any statesman or lawgiver can do for him. The statesman who should attempt to direct private people in what manner they ought to employ their capitals would not only load himself with a most unnecessary attention, but assume an authority which could safely be trusted, not only to no single person, but to no council or senate whatever, and which would nowhere be so dangerous as in the hands of a man who had folly and presumption enough to fancy himself fit to exercise it.

To give the monopoly of the home market to the produce of domestic industry, in any particular art or manufacture, is in some measure to direct private people in what manner they ought to employ their capitals, and must, in almost all cases, be either a useless or a hurtful regulation. If the produce of domestic can be brought there as cheap as that of foreign industry, the regulation is evidently useless. If it cannot, it must generally be hurtful. It is the maxim of every prudent master of a family never to attempt to make at home what it will cost him more to make than to buy. The tailor does not attempt to make his own shoes, but buys them of the shoemaker. The shoemaker does not attempt to make his own clothes, but employs a tailor. The farmer attempts to make neither the one nor the other, but employs those different artificers. All of them find it for their interest to employ their whole industry in a way in which they have some advantage over their neighbours, and to purchase with a part of its produce, or what is the same thing, with the price of a part of it, whatever else they have occasion for.

What is prudence in the conduct of every private family can scarce be folly in that of a great kingdom. If a foreign country can supply us with a commodity cheaper than we ourselves can make it, better buy it of them with some part of the produce of our own industry employed in a way in which we have some advantage.

WN 423, 424

In the midst of all the exactions of government, this capital has been silently and gradually accumulated by the private frugality and good conduct of individuals, by their universal, continual, and uninterrupted effort to better their own condition. It is this effort, protected by law and allowed by liberty to exert itself in the manner that is most advantageous, which has maintained the progress of England towards opulence and improvement in almost all former times, and which, it is to be hoped, will do so in all future times. England, however, as it has never been blessed with a very parsimonious government, so parsimony has at no time been the characteristical virtue of its inhabitants. It is the highest impertinence and presumption, therefore, in kings and ministers, to pretend to watch over the economy of private people, and to restrain their expense, either by sumptuary laws, or by prohibiting the importation of foreign luxuries. They are themselves always, and without any exception, the greatest spendthrifts in the society. Let them look well after their own expense, and they may safely trust private people with theirs. If their own extravagance does not ruin the state, that of their subjects never will.

WN 328, 329

Frugality and good conduct, however, is upon most occasions, it appears from experience, sufficient to compensate, not only the private prodigality and misconduct of individuals, but the public extravagance of government. The uniform, constant, and uninterrupted effort of every man to better his condition, the principle from which public and national, as well as private opulence is originally derived, is frequently powerful enough to maintain the natural progress of things towards improvement, in spite both of the extravagance of government, and of the greatest errors of administration. Like the unknown principle of animal life, it frequently restores health and vigour to the constitution, in spite, not only of the disease, but of the absurd prescriptions of the doctor.

WN 326

23

Law and Justice

If there is any society among robbers and murderers, they must at least, according to the trite observation, abstain from robbing and murdering one another. Beneficence, therefore, is less essential to the existence of society than justice. Society may subsist, though not in the most comfortable state, without beneficence; but the prevalence of injustice must utterly destroy it.

MS 167

Though nature, therefore, exhorts mankind to acts of beneficence, by the pleasing consciousness of deserved reward, she has not thought it necessary to guard and enforce the practice of it by the terrors of merited punishment in case it should be neglected. It is the ornament which embellishes, not the foundation which supports the building, and which it was, therefore, sufficient to recommend, but by no means necessary to impose. Justice, on the contrary, is the main pillar that upholds the whole edifice. If it is removed, the great, the immense fabric of human society, that fabric which, to raise and support, seems, in this world, if I may say so, to have been the peculiar and darling care of nature, must in a moment crumble into atoms. In order to enforce the observation of justice, therefore, nature has implanted in the human breast that consciousness of ill desert, those terrors of merited punishment, which attend upon its violation, as the great safeguards of the association of mankind, to protect the weak, to curb the violent, and to chastise the guilty.

Men, though naturally sympathetic, feel so little for another, with whom they have no particular connection, in comparison of what they feel for themselves; the misery of one, who is merely their fellow-creature, is of so little importance to them in comparison even of a small conveniency of their own; they have it so much in their power to hurt him, and may have so many temptations to do so, that if this principle did not stand up within them in his defence, and overawe them into a respect for his innocence, they would, like wild beasts, be at all times ready to fly upon him; and a man would enter an assembly of men as he enters a den of lions.

MS 167, 168

Mere justice is, upon most occasions, but a negative virtue, and only hinders us from hurting our neighbour.

The man who barely abstains from violating either the person or the estate, or the reputation, of his neighbours, has surely very little positive merit. He fulfils, however, all the rules of what is peculiarly called justice, and does every thing which his equals can with propriety force him to do, or which they can punish him for not doing. We may often fulfil all the rules of justice by sitting still and doing nothing.

MS 160

The violation of justice is injury: it does real and positive hurt to some particular persons, from motives which are naturally disapproved of. It is, therefore, the proper object of resentment, and of punishment, which is the natural consequence of resentment. As mankind go along with, and approve of, the violence employed to avenge the hurt which is done by injustice, so they much more go along with, and approve of, that which is employed to prevent and beat off the injury, and to restrain the offender from hurting his neighbours. The person himself who meditates an injustice is sensible of this, and feels that force may, with the utmost propriety, be made use of, both by the person whom he is about to injure, and by others, either to obstruct the execution of his crime, or to punish him when he has executed it. And upon this is founded that remarkable distinction between justice and all the other social virtues, which has of late been particularly insisted upon by an author of very great and original genius, that we feel ourselves to be under a stricter obligation to act according to justice, than agreeably to friendship, charity, or generosity; that the practice of these last-mentioned virtues seem to be left in some measure to our own choice, but that, somehow or other, we feel ourselves to be in a peculiar manner tied, bound, and obliged, to the observation of justice.

We feel, that is to say, that force may, with the utmost propriety, and with the approbation of all mankind, be made use of to constrain us to observe the rules of the one, but not to follow the precepts of the other.

MS 157

To scourge a person of quality, or to set him in the pillory, upon account of any crime whatever, is a brutality of which no European government, except that of Russia, is capable.

MS 124

Death is the greatest evil which one man can inflict upon another, and excites the highest degree of resentment in those who are immediately connected with the slain. Murder, therefore, is the most atrocious of all crimes which affect individuals only, in the sight both of mankind and of the person who has committed it. To be deprived of that which we are possessed of, is a greater evil than to be disappointed of what we have only the expectation. Breach of property, therefore, theft and robbery, which take from us what we are possessed of, are greater crimes than breach of contract, which only disappoints us of what we expected. The most sacred laws of justice, therefore, those whose violation seems to call loudest for vengeance and punishment, are the laws which guard the life and person of our neighbour; the next are those which guard his property and possessions; and last of all come those which guard what are called his personal rights, or what is due to him from the promises of others.

MS 163

The rules of justice may be compared to the rules of grammar; the rules of the other virtues to the rules which critics lay down for the attainment of what is sublime and elegant in composition. The one are precise, accurate, and indispensable. The other are loose, vague, and indeterminate, and present us rather with a general idea of the perfection we ought to aim at, than afford us any certain and infallible directions for acquiring it. A man may learn to write grammatically by rule, with the most absolute infallibility; and so, perhaps, he may be taught to act justly. But there are no rules whose observance will infallibly lead us to the attainment of elegance or sublimity in writing: though there are some which may help us, in some measure, to correct and ascertain the vague ideas which we might otherwise have entertained of those perfections; And there are no rules by the knowledge of which we can infallibly be taught to act upon all occasions with prudence, with just magnanimity, or proper beneficence; though there are some which may enable us to correct and ascertain, in several respects, the imperfect ideas which we might otherwise have entertained of those virtues.

MS 290

When the judicial is united to the executive power, it is scarce possible that justice should not frequently be sacrificed to what is vulgarly called politics. The persons entrusted with the great interests of the state may, even without any corrupt view, sometimes imagine it necessary to sacrifice to those interests the rights of a private man. But upon the impartial administration of justice depends the liberty of every individual, the sense which he has of his own security. In order to make every individual feel himself perfectly secure in the possession of every right which belongs to him, it is not only necessary that the judicial should be separated from the executive power, but that it should be rendered as much as possible independent of that power. The judge should not be liable to be removed from his office according to the caprice of that power. The regular payment of his salary should not depend upon the good-will or even upon the good economy of that power.

WN 681

It had been the custom in modern Europe to regulate, upon most occasions, the payment of the attornies and clerks of court, according to the number of pages which they had occasion to write; the court, however, requiring that each page should contain so many lines, and each line so many words. In order to increase their payment, the attornies and clerks had contrived to multiply words beyond all necessity, to the corruption of the law language of, I believe, every court of justice in Europe. A like temptation might perhaps occasion a like corruption in the form of law proceedings.

WN 680

In no country do the decisions of positive law coincide exactly, in every case, with the rules which the natural sense of justice would dictate. Systems of positive law, therefore, though they deserve the greatest authority, as the records of the sentiments of mankind in different ages and nations, yet can never be regarded as accurate systems of the rules of natural justice.

MS 536

In those corrupted governments where there is at least a general suspicion of much unnecessary expense, and great misapplication of the public revenue, the laws which regard it are little respected. Not many people are scrupulous about smuggling when, without perjury, they can find any easy and safe opportunity of doing so. To pretend to have any scruple about buying smuggled goods, though a manifest encouragement to the violation of the revenue laws, and to the perjury which almost always attends it, would in most countries be regarded as one of those pedantic pieces of hypocrisy which, instead of gaining credit with anybody, serve only to expose the person who affects to practice them to the suspicion of being a greater knave than most of his neighbours. By this indulgence of the public, the smuggler is often encouraged to continue a trade which he is thus taught to consider as in some measure innocent, and when the severity of the revenue laws is ready to fall upon him, he is frequently disposed to defend with violence what he has been accustomed to regard as his just property. From being at first, perhaps, rather imprudent than criminal, he at last too often becomes one of the hardiest and most determined violators of the laws of society. By the ruin of the smuggler, his capital, which had before been employed in maintaining productive labour, is absorbed either in the revenue of the state or in that of the revenue officer, and is employed in maintaining unproductive, to the diminution of the general capital of the society and of the useful industry which it might otherwise have maintained.

WN 849

If I owe a man ten pounds, justice requires that I should pay him precisely ten pounds, either at the time agreed upon, or when he demands it. What I ought to perform, how much I ought to perform, when and where I ought to perform it, the whole nature and circumstance of the action prescribed, are all of them precisely fixed and determined. Though it may be awkward and pedantic, therefore, to affect too strict an adherence to the common

rules of prudence and generosity, there is no pedantry in
sticking fast by the rules of justice.

MS 289

To restrain private people, it may be said, from receiving in payment the promissory notes of a banker, for any
sum whether great or small, when they themselves are
willing to receive them, or to restrain a banker from issu-
ing such notes, whan all his neighbours are willing to
accept of them, is a manifest violation of that natural
liberty which it is the proper business of law not to in-
fringe, but to support. Such regulations may, no doubt,
be considered as in some respects a violation of natural
liberty. But those exertions of the natural liberty of a few
individuals, which might endanger the security of the
whole society, are, and ought to be, restrained by the
laws of all governments, of the most free as well as of the
most despotical. The obligation of building party walls,
in order to prevent the communication of fire, is a violation of natural liberty exactly of the same kind with the
regulations of the banking trade which are here proposed.

WN 308

The laws concerning corn may every where be compared to the laws concerning religion. The people feel
themselves so much interested in what relates either to
their subsistence in this life, or to their happiness in a life
to come, that government must yield to their prejudices,

and, in order to preserve the public tranquillity, establish that system which they approve of.

WN 507

Commerce and manufactures can seldom flourish long in any state which does not enjoy a regular administration of justice, in which the people do not feel themselves secure in the possession of their property, in which the faith of contracts is not supported by law, and in which the authority of the state is not supposed to be regularly employed in enforcing the payment of debts from all those who are able to pay. Commerce and manufactures, in short, can seldom flourish in any state in which there is not a certain degree of confidence in the justice of government.

WN 862

24

Man and Society

Political economy, considered as a branch of the science of a statesman or legislator, proposes two distinct objects: first, to provide a plentiful revenue or subsistence for the people, or more properly to enable them to provide such a revenue or subsistence for themselves; and secondly, to supply the state or commonwealth with a revenue sufficient for the public services. It proposes to enrich both the people and the sovereign.

WN 297

Every man is rich or poor according to the degree in which he can afford to enjoy the necessaries, conveniences, and amusements of human life.

WN 30

The progressive state is in reality the cheerful and the

hearty state to all the different orders of the society. The stationary is dull; the declining melancholy.

WN 81

Is this improvement in the circumstances of the lower ranks of the people to be regarded as an advantage or as an inconveniency to the society? The answer seems at first sight abundantly plain. Servants, labourers, and workmen of different kinds, make up the far greater part of every great political society. But what improves the circumstances of the great part can never be regarded as an inconveniency to the whole. No society can surely be flourishing and happy, of which the far greater part of the members are poor and miserable. It is but equity, besides, that they who feed, clothe, and lodge the whole body of the people, should have such a share of the produce of their own labour as to be themselves tolerably well fed, clothed and lodged.

WN 78, 79

In the progress of the division of labour, the employment of the far greater part of those who live by labour, that is, of the great body of the people, comes to be confined to a few very simple operations, frequently to one or two. But the understandings of the greater part of men are necessarily formed by their ordinary employments. The man whose whole life is spent in performing a few simple operations, of which the effects are perhaps always the same, or very nearly the same, has no occasion to exert his understanding or to exercise his invention in finding out expedients for removing difficulties which never occur. He naturally loses, therefore, the habit of such exertion, and generally becomes as stupid and ignorant as it is possible for a human creature to become. The torpor of his mind renders him not only incapable of relishing or bearing a part in any rational conversation, but of conceiving any generous, noble, or tender sentiment, and consequently of forming any just judgment concerning many even of the ordinary duties of private life.

WN 734, 735

It is in the progressive state, while the society is advancing to the further acquisition, rather than when it has acquired its full complement of riches, that the condition of the labouring poor, of the great body of the people, seems to be the happiest and the most comfortable. It is hard in the stationary, and miserable in the declining state.

WN 81

Birth and fortune are evidently the two circumstances which principally set one man above another. They are the two great sources of personal distinction, and are therefore the principal causes which naturally establish authority and subordination among men.

WN 673

Though the state was to derive no advantage from the instruction of the inferior ranks of people, it would still deserve its attention that they should not be altogether uninstructed. The state, however, derives no inconsiderable advantage from their instruction. The more they are instructed the less liable they are to the delusions of enthusiasm and superstition, which, among ignorant nations, frequently occasion the most dreadful disorders. An instructed and intelligent people, besides, are always more decent and orderly than an ignorant and stupid one.

WN 739, 740

Merchants and master manufacturers are, in this order, the two classes of people who commonly employ the largest capitals, and who by their wealth draw to themselves the greatest share of the public consideration. As during their whole lives they are engaged in plans and projects, they have frequently more acuteness of understanding than the greater part of country gentlemen. As their thoughts, however, are commonly exercised rather about the interest of their own particular branch of business, than about that of the society, their judgment, even when given with the greatest candour (which it has not been upon every occasion) is much more to be depended upon with regard to the former of those two objects than with regard to the latter. Their superiority over the country gentleman is not so much in their knowledge of their own interest that they have frequently imposed upon his generosity, and persuaded him to give up both his own interest and that of the public, from a very simple but honest conviction that their interest, and not his, was the interest of the public. The interest of the dealers, however, in any particular branch of trade of manufactures, is always in some respects different from, and even opposite to, that of the public. To widen the market and to narrow the competition, is always the interest of the dealers. To widen the market may frequently be agreeable enough to the interest of the public; but to narrow the competition must always be against it, and can serve only to enable the dealers, by raising their profits above what they naturally would be, to levy, for their own benefit, an absurd tax upon the rest of their fellow-citizens. The proposal of any new law or regulation of commerce which comes from this order ought always to be listened to with great precaution, and ought never to be adopted till after having been long and carefully examined, not only with the most scrupulous, but with the most suspicious attention. It comes from an order of men whose interest is never exactly the same with that of the public, who have generally an interest to deceive and even to oppress the public, and who accordingly have, upon many occasions, both deceived and oppressed it.

WN 250

Men of inferior wealth combine to defend those of superior wealth in the possession of their property, in order that men of superior wealth may combine to defend them in the possession of theirs.

WN 674

We rarely hear, it has been said, of the combinations of masters, though frequently of those of workmen. But whoever imagines, upon this account, that masters rarely combine, is as ignorant of the world as of the subject. Masters are always and everywhere in a sort of tacit, but constant and uniform combination, not to raise the wages of labour above their actual rate. To violate this combination is everywhere a most unpopular action, and a sort of reproach to a master among his neighbours and equals. We seldom, indeed, hear of this combination, because it is the usual, and one may say, the natural state of things, which nobody ever hears of. Masters, too, sometimes enter into particular combinations to sink the wages of labour even below this rate. These are always conducted with the utmost silence and secrecy, till the moment of execution, and when the workmen yield, as they sometimes do, without resistance, though severely felt by them, they are never heard of by other people. Such combinations, however, are frequently resisted by a contrary defensive combination of the workmen; who sometimes too, without any provocation of this kind, combine of their own accord to raise the price of their labour. Their usual pretences are, sometimes the high price of provisions; sometimes the great profit which their masters make by their work. But whether their combinations be offensive or defensive, they are always abundantly heard of. In order to bring the point to a speedy decision, they have always recourse to the loudest clamour, and sometimes to the most shocking violence and outrage. They are desperate, and act with the folly and extravagance of desperate men, who must either starve, or frighten their masters into an immediate compliance with their demands. The masters upon these occasions are just as clamorous upon the other side, and never cease to call aloud for the assistance of the civil magistrate, and the rigorous execution of those laws which have been enacted with so much severity against the combination of servants, labourers, and journeymen. The workmen, accordingly, very seldom derive any advantage from the violence of those tumultuous combinations, which, partly from the interposition of the civil magistrate, partly from the superior steadiness of the masters, partly from the necessity which the greater part of the workmen are under of submitting for the sake of present subsistence, generally end in nothing, but the punishment or ruin of the ringleaders.

WN 66, 67

Excessive application during four days of the week is frequently the real cause of the idleness of the other three, so much and so loudly complained of. Great labour, either of mind or body, continued for several days together, is in most men naturally followed by a great desire of relaxation, which, if not restrained by force or by some strong necessity, is almost irresistible. It is the call of nature, which requires to be relieved by some indulgence, sometimes of ease only, but sometimes, too, of dissipation and diversion. If it is not complied with, the consequences are often dangerous, and sometimes fatal, and such as almost always, sooner or later, bring on the peculiar infirmity of the trade. If masters would always listen to the dictates of reason and humanity, they have frequently occasion rather to moderate than to animate the application of many of their workmen. It will be found, I believe, in every sort of trade, that the man who works so moderately as to be able to work constantly not only preserves his health the longest, but, in the course of the year, executes the greatest quantity of work.

WN 82

Whatever, therefore, we may imagine the real wealth and revenue of a country to consist in, whether in the value of the annual produce of its land and labour, as plain reason seems to dictate; or in the quantity of the precious metals which circulate within it, as vulgar prejudices suppose; in either view of the matter, every prodigal appears to be a public enemy, and every frugal man a public benefactor.

WN 324

It can seldom happen, indeed, that the circumstances of a great nation can be much affected either by the prodigality or misconduct of individuals; the profusion or imprudence of some, being always more than compensated by the frugality and good conduct of others.

WN 324

With regard to profusion, the principle which prompts to expense, is the passion for present enjoyment; which, though sometimes violent and very difficult to be restrained, is in general only momentary and occasional. But the principle which prompts to save, is the desire of bettering our condition, a desire which, though generally calm and dispassionate, comes with us from the womb, and never leaves us till we go into the grave. In the whole interval which separates those two moments, there is scarce perhaps a single instant in which any man is so perfectly and completely satisfied with his situation, as to be without any wish of alteration or improvement of any kind. An augmentation of fortune is the means by which the greater part of men propose and wish to better their condition. It is the means the most vulgar and the most obvious; and the most likely way of augmenting their fortune, is to save and accumulate some part of what they acquire, either regularly and annually, or upon some extraordinary occasions. Though the principle of expense, therefore prevails in almost all men upon some occasions, and in some men upon almost all occasions, yet in the greater part of men, taking the whole course of their life at an average, the principle of frugality seems not only to predominate but to predominate very greatly.

WN 324, 325

Great nations are never impoverished by private, though they sometimes are by public prodigality and misconduct. The whole, or almost the whole public revenue, is in most countries employed in maintaining unproductive hands. Such are the people who compose a numerous and splendid court, a great ecclesiastical establishment, great fleets and armies, who in time of peace produce nothing, and in time of war acquire nothing which can compensate the expense of maintaining them, even while the war lasts. Such people, as they themselves produce nothing, are all maintained by the produce of other men's labour.

WN 325

The man who borrows in order to spend will soon be ruined, and he who lends to him will generally have occasion to repent of his folly. To borrow or to lend for such a purpose, therefore, is in all cases, where gross usury is out of the question, contrary to the interest of both parties; and though it no doubt happens sometimes that people do both the one and the other; yet, from the regard that all men have for their own interest, we may be assured, that it cannot happen so very frequently as we are sometimes apt to imagine. Ask any rich man of common prudence, to which of the two sorts of people he has lent the greater part of his stock, to those who, he thinks, will employ it profitably, or to those who will spend it idly, and he will laugh at you for proposing the question. Even among borrowers, therefore, not the people in the world most famous for frugality, the number of the frugal and industrious surpasses considerably that of the prodigal and idle.

WN 333

If the prodigality of some was not compensated by the frugality of others, the conduct of every prodigal, by feeding the idle with the bread of the industrious, tends not only to beggar himself, but to impoverish his country.

WN 322

The houses, the furniture, the clothing of the rich, in a little time, become useful to the inferior and middling ranks of people. They are able to purchase then when their superiors grow weary of them, and the general accommodation of the whole people is thus gradually improved, when this mode of expense becomes universal among men of fortune. In countries which have long been rich, you will frequently find the inferior ranks of people in possession both of houses and furniture perfectly good and entire, but of which neither the one could have been built, nor the other have been made for their use. What was formerly a seat of the family of Seymour, is now an inn upon the Bath road. The marriage-bed of James the First of Great Britain, which his Queen brought with her from Denmark, as a present fit for a sovereign to make to a sovereign, was, a few years ago, the ornament of an ale-house at Dunfermline.

WN 329, 330

A person who can acquire no property, can have no other interest but to eat as much, and to labour as little as possible. Whatever work he does beyond what is sufficient to purchase his own maintenance, can be squeezed out of him by violence only, and not by any interest of his own.

WN 365

Nature, when she formed man for society, endowed him with an original desire to please, and an original aversion to offend his brethren. She taught him to feel pleasure in their favourable, and pain in their unfavourable regard. She rendered their approbation most flattering and most agreeable to him for its own sake; and their disapprobation most mortifying and most offensive.

MS 212

It is not because one man keeps a coach while his neighbour walks a-foot that the one is rich and the other poor; but because the one is rich he keeps a coach, and because the other is poor he walks a-foot.

WN 76

What can be added to the happiness of the man who is in health, who is out of debt, and has a clear conscience? To one in this situation all accessions of fortune may properly be said to be superflous; and if he is much elevated upon account of them, it must be the effect of the most frivolous levity. This situation, however, may very well be called the natural and ordinary state of mankind. Notwithstanding the present misery and depravity of the world, so justly lamented, this really is the state of the greater part of men.

MS 105

Nothing tends so much to promote public spirit as the study of politics, — of the several systems of civil government, their advantages and disadvantages, — of the constitution of our own country, its situation, and interest with regard to foreign nations, its commerce, its defence, the disadvantages it labours under, the dangers to which it may be exposed, how to remove the one, and how to guard against the other. Upon this account political disquisitions, if just, and reasonable, and practicable, are of all the works of speculation the most useful. Even the weakest and the worst of them are not altogether without their utility. They serve at least to animate the public passions of men, and rouse them to seek out the means of promoting the happiness of the society.

MS 307

Men of no more than ordinary discernment never rate any person higher than he appears to rate himself. He seems doubtful himself, they say, whether he is perfectly fit for such a situation or such an office, and immediately give the preference to some impudent blockhead who entertains no doubt about his own qualifications.

MS 418

A true party-man hates and despises candour; and, in reality, there is no vice which could so effectually disqualify him for the trade of a party-man as that single virtue. The real, revered, and impartial spectator, therefore, is upon no occasion at a greater distance than amidst the violence and rage of contending parties. To them it may be said, that such a spectator scarce exists anywhere in the universe. Even to the great Judge of the universe they impute all their own prejudices and often view that divine Being as animated by all their own vindictive and implacable passions. Of all the corrupters of moral sentiments, therefore, faction and fanaticism have always been by far the greatest.

MS 259, 260

Rebels and heretics are those unlucky persons, who, when things have come to a certain degree of violence, have the misfortune to be of the weaker party.

MS 259

Amidst the turbulence and disorder of faction, a certain spirit of system is apt to mix itself with that public spirit which is founded upon the love of humanity, upon a real fellow-feeling with the inconveniencies and distresses to which some of our fellow-citizens may be exposed. This spirit of system commonly takes the direction of that more gentle public spirit, always animates it, and often inflames it, even to the madness of fanaticism. The leaders of the discontented party seldom fail to hold out some plausible plan of reformation, which, they pretend, will not only remove the inconveniencies and relieve the distresses immediately complained of, but will prevent in all times coming any return of the like inconveniencies and distresses. They often propose, upon this account, to new-model the constitution, and to alter in some of its most essential parts that system of government under which the subjects of a great empire have enjoyed, perhaps, peace, security, and even glory, during the course of several centuries together. The great body of the party are commonly intoxicated with the imaginary beauty of this ideal system, of which they have no experience, but which has been represented to them in all the most dazzling colours in which the eloquence of their leaders could paint it. Those leaders themselves, though they originally may have meant nothing but their own aggrandizement, become, many of them, in time the dupes of their own sophistry, and are as eager for this great reformation as the weakest and foolishest of their followers.

MS 379

The man whose public spirit is prompted altogether by humanity and benevolence, will respect the established powers and privileges even of individuals, and still more those of the great orders and societies into which the state is divided. Though he should consider some of them as in some measure abusive, he will content himself with moderating, what he often cannot annihilate without great violence. When he can not conquer the rooted prejudices of the people by reason and persuasion, he will not attempt to subdue them by force, but will religiously observe what by Cicero is justly called the divine maxim of Plato, never to use violence to his country, no more than to his parents. He will accommodate, as well as he can, his public arrangements to the confirmed habits and prejudices of the people, and will remedy, as well as he can, the inconveniencies which may flow from the want of those regulations which the people are averse to submit to. When he cannot establish the right, he will not disdain to ameliorate the wrong; but, like Solon, when he cannot establish the best system of laws he will endeavour to establish the best that the people can bear.

The man of system, on the contrary, is apt to be very wise in his own conceit, and is often so enamoured with the supposed beauty of his own ideal plan of government, that he cannot suffer the smallest deviation from any part of it. He goes on to establish it completely and in all its parts, without any regard either to the great interests or to the strong prejudices which may oppose it: he seems to imagine that he can arrange the different members of a great society with as much ease as the hand arranges the different pieces upon a chess-board; he does not consider that the pieces upon the chess-board have no other principle of motion besides that which the hand impresses upon them; but that in the great chess-board of human society, every single piece has a principle of motion of its own, altogether different from that which the legislature might choose to impress upon it. If those two principles coincide and act in tl.e same direction, the game of human society will go on easily and harmoniously, and is very likely to be happy and successful. If they are opposite or different, the game will go on miserably, and the society must be at all times in the highest degree of disorder.

MS 380, 381

The natural effort of every individual to better his own condition, when suffered to exert itself with freedom and security, is so powerful a principle, that it is alone, and without any assistance, not only capable of carrying on the society to wealth and prosperity, but of surmounting a hundred impertinent obstructions with which the folly of human laws too often incumbers its operations.

WN 508

Index

This book was photoset in the Times Roman series of type. The face was designed to be used in the news columns of the *London Times*. The *Times* was seeking a type face that would be condensed enough to accommodate a substantial number of words per column without sacrificing readability and still have an attractive, contemporary appearance. This design was an immediate success. It is used in many periodicals throughout the world and is one of the most popular text faces presently in use for book work.

This book is printed on 70-pound long-fibre, acid-free paper especially developed by the S. D. Warren Company to meet the historical document standards of the United States National Historical Publications and Records Commission.

Book design by Design Center, Inc., Indianapolis
Typography and printing by the North Central Publishing Co., Saint Paul